an UNCOMMON guide to Minnesota

by Nina McGuire
and Barbara Budd

A Tailored Tours Publication

Viking Press Inc., Minneapolis, Minnesota

By the same authors

An Uncommon Guide to the Twin Cities

ACKNOWLEDGEMENTS

We wish to express our gratitude to many
friends who have so willingly shared their
knowledge of Minnesota with us. They have been
most generous.

Without the following organizations, this
book could not have been written. We gratefully
acknowledge their cooperation, their research
facilities, and their encouragement.

The Minnesota Conservation Department
The Minnesota Office of Economic Development
The Minnesota Historical Society
The Minnesota Highway Department
The U.S. Department of Federal Parks

We have visited with many Chamber of
Commerce members throughout the state. Without
exception, they have been most gracious in pro-
viding background information and materials
concerning specific areas.

We offer special thanks to our husbands and
Betsey, Jay, Peter, Ben, Douglas, and Stuart,
our children. Their enthusiasm for this project,
their impressions throughout our travels, and
their pleasure in our pleasure have brought you
this book.

Although many have helped, the final book
is our responsibility alone. No gratuities or
other considerations have been received from any
establishment mentioned. Our criteria was to
select only those facilities which TO US were
unique and outstanding in their category.

We wish you happy adventures throughout
MINNESOTA.

TABLE
OF
CONTENTS

WELCOME

Welcome to Minnesota, a land of lakes and sky blue water! We have had a marvelous time learning about and exploring our state. We invite you to join us for some fun-filled visits through Minnesota's past, some projections concerning the future, and an adventuresome outing within the present day state.

Minnesota has cosmopolitan cities and wilderness canoe areas, iron mines and fields of waving wheat, an international seaport and a medical metropolis. The nation's largest lake touches Minnesota shores and the third longest river in the world begins in one of the state's forests as a rippling stream.

Although Chippewa and Sioux Indian tribes lived in this area for centuries, intense white settlement began only a little over a hundred years ago. Pioneers came from the east, the south, from Canada and from Europe. The soil was fertile and, soon, a land of small farms sprouted from the wilderness. Homesteaders worked hard and were extremely self-reliant. These qualities have carried to their children and grandchildren. And yet, the hard work has not dulled a Minnesotan's love for fun. Parties and festivals and fairs punctuate the seasons. Visitors are always welcome to share the good times.

Education, at all levels, is exceedingly important here. Many educators believe that the quality of graduating students has had much to do with Minnesota's emergence as a leading electronics, agricultural, and financial center for middle America. Milling, mining, and tourism also contribute to the state's healthy economic climate.

Fishing poles, snowmobiles, canoes, sailboats, golf clubs, camping gear, and skis are but a few examples of the Minnesotan's continuing love affair with his outdoor world.

Minnesota's people, her places, her beauty beckon you to come exploring! You are welcome here!

FUN FOR
YOUNG AND
OLD

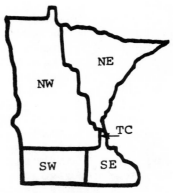

Come with us and
enjoy the wonderful
happenings through-
out Minnesota!

We have divided the
state into 5
sections:

Northeastern Minnesota (NE)
Northwestern Minnesota (NW)
Twin Cities (TC)
Southeastern Minnesota (SE)
Southwestern Minnesota (SW)

Northeastern Minnesota

This is a land of wilderness and variety.
Within the following tours, we acquaint you
with Minnesota's northeastern past, you explore
an international seaport, and travel "out to
sea" to one of the state's most interesting
islands.

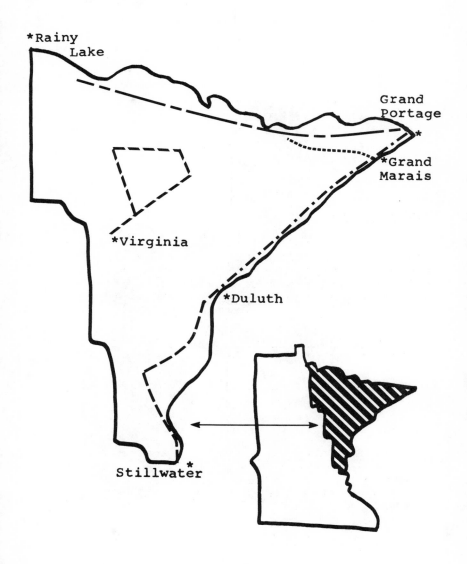

*Rainy
Lake

Grand
Portage
*

*Grand
Marais

*Virginia

*Duluth

Stillwater *

*International Falls
   *Rainy
     Lake   BOUNDARY WATERS
                     CANOE AREA

VOYAGEUR
NATIONAL
PARK
                   *Crooked
                    Lake
                 SUPERIOR NATIONAL   Grand*
                      FOREST   Portage
            Ely*   *Voyageur Visitor
                       Center

Come vacation beyond civilization.

Today's traveller along the inland waterways
will see a world that is very similar to that
canoed 600 years ago by the Chippewa Indians--or
200 years ago by the lusty French Canadian fur
traders (Voyageurs). Minnesotans have preserved
one of their most significant assets, the
wilderness.

Ely's streets are lined with outfitters to
help today's explorer return to the woods and
lakes. Canoe trip outfitters are also head-
quartered in Grand Marais and Duluth.

Excellent descriptive information is available, free of charge, from the Forest Supervisor,
Superior National Forest, Box 338, Duluth,
Minnesota. The United States Geological Survey,
Washington, D.C. produces topographical maps of
the Boundary Waters Canoe Area (BWCA). They
cost about 50¢ and provide an opportunity for
"armchair exploring" before dipping paddles into
that special world of lakes and pines.

Canoeists will enjoy reviewing a few
books before exploring Minnesota's magnificent
wilderness areas. We strongly recommend that
the novice borrow or buy the following before
a trip north.

The Sierra Club Wilderness Handbook
Ballantine Books, N.Y. Paperback 75¢

Canoeing, The American Red Cross,
Washington, D.C. Paperback $1.50

Join us in the following pages as we trace
one of the Voyageur's routes through what is now
a beautiful section of Minnesota.

NE-Voyageur Visitor Center-Ely

A visit to the <u>Voyageur Visitor Center</u> helps recall the adventure-filled lives of the French Canadian fur traders. Children marvel at the giant birchbark canoe in which 5 or 6 men transported loads of more than 5 tons of fur along the inland waterway toward Grand Portage. The exhibits within the museum are excellent. They provide today's wilderness traveller with visual reminders of yesterday's world.

Location: 1/2 mile east of Ely on Hwy. 169
Hours: Open during the summer months from 9 am to 6 pm
Fees: Free
Note: Family-oriented films are shown each summer evening at 7:30 pm. They are free.

All persons canoeing within the Boundary Waters Canoe Area (BWCA) are <u>required</u> to obtain a free permit from the Superior Forest Office near the Voyageur Visitor Center. The permit is for your protection and for the protection of the wilderness. Strict regulations go into effect in 1971 prohibiting metal and other potential waste products within the BWCA. Canoe routes and portage (places where canoes must be carried) information is provided. There are only a few places where a motor may be used. The BWCA contains over 1200 miles of canoe routes, campgrounds are available throughout the area, and the fishing is excellent.

As you approach the access route to the BWCA, plan to stop in <u>Ely</u> "Canoe Capital of the World". This little town probably contains more canoeing experts than any other place in America. The outfitters share their enthusiasm for the lakeland. We know many people who explored Ely "just for fun" and returned the next year to become avid canoeists.

Watching for <u>pictographs</u> is a superb way to spend an afternoon. These colorful, primitive drawings were made by Indians between 600 and 800 years ago. Usually outlined in red, the pictographs appear a few feet above the water line on rock outcroppings. (Keep watching for the pipe smoking moose on Crooked Lake. Friends insist it's really there.)

Location: Throughout the BWCA, but particularly at Crooked Lake, Darky Lake and Agnes Lake

While within the BWCA, stop and explore a <u>deserted island</u>. Islands often served as meeting stations for the Voyageurs and Indians. Although it is unlikely, you may find some traces of these men as you silently glide into their world.

On January 8, 1971 the <u>Voyageurs National</u> Park was born. This 219,000 acre wilderness shall be preserved with only limited road access. It greatly expands the range of waterworld activities. Non-canoeists might enjoy a visit to <u>Rainy Lake</u> where houseboats are popular and available for rental.

Location: <u>Rainy Lake</u> is northeast of International Falls on the Minnesota-Canada border.

NE-Grand Portage National Monument

The Voyageur's trading season ended with a BIG party! Indians and traders met at <u>Grand Portage</u> each year for a colossal celebration. After days of near riotous merrymaking, the Voyageurs headed out across Lake Superior to deliver tons of pelts to the large fur company headquarters. The Indians returned to the silence of their forests to begin the next year's trapping.

<u>Grand Portage National Monument</u> remains as a silent memorial to another century. There is a small museum and a number of beautiful, well-marked trails to explore. It also marks the beginning of a 9 mile portage (carry) for canoeists entering the inland waterway.

Location: Route 61, Grand Portage National
            Monument
Hours: Daily
Fees: Free

You can tell an avid northwoods canoeist by his ability to carry his canoe for 9 miles from Grand Portage to the beginning of the inland waterway. It has been said that canoeing is a beautiful way to be in touch with nature, that it can be romantic, and that it can be a lot of hard work! All three are true at times!

The distance between
<u>Stillwater</u> and
<u>Duluth</u> is approximately
150 miles.

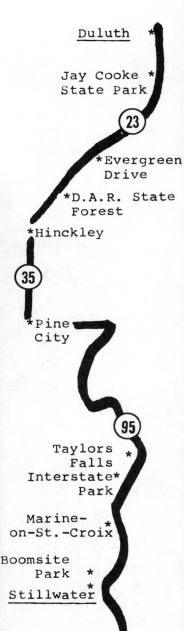

<u>Duluth</u> *

Jay Cooke *
State Park

(23)

*Evergreen
Drive

*D.A.R. State
Forest

*Hinckley

(35)

*Pine
City

(95)

Taylors *
Falls
Interstate*
Park

Marine- *
on-St.-Croix

Boomsite
Park *
*
<u>Stillwater</u>*

*Twin
Cities

16

TIMBER.   TIM-BER!

For years this cry rang through the virgin
forests near the St. Croix River. As settlers
moved West, wood was needed to build the houses
and towns that would emerge in the Minnesota
territory. The word was passed and logging
camps were soon filled with the baudy, boisterous,
larger-than-life lumberjacks.

Stillwater is Minnesota's oldest city.   It
began as a sawmill town. Her hill is still lined
with mansions built by early lumber barons.
The Warden's House Museum contains an interesting
collection of early lumbering artifacts, as well
as antique prison equipment.

Location: 602 N. Main St., Stillwater
Hours: May 1-November 1 on Tuesdays,
            Thursdays, Saturdays and Sun-
            days from 2-5 pm
Fees: Adults (25¢), children (10¢)

Clear water, sandy island beaches, an easy
current--all this and more combine to make the
St. Croix one of America's loveliest "pleasure"
rivers.

As today's tourist enjoys the beauty of the
river, it is interesting to recall that the
scene was very different in the 1800s. At
Boomsite Park millions of logs were sorted,
scaled, measured, and rafted down river to the
mills in Stillwater. Over 15,000,000 feet of
lumber went through this boom site.

Location: 1 mi. north of Stillwater on
            Rt. 95
Note: If you have your own boat, this
            park serves as an access point
            for the St. Croix.

Marine-on-St. Croix with its white frame houses serves as another reminder of the area's lumbering days. The Museum is a restored townhouse and jail. The doll collection fascinates little girls while many not so little girls explore the early Swedish-American kitchen.

      Location: 2 blocks west of Hwy. 95
      Hours: Summer months only on Saturdays
                  and Sundays from 2-5 pm
      Fees: Donations accepted

Be sure to see the 60 foot deep pot holes at Interstate Park. These "holes" were formed over 11,000 years ago when the melting glaciers rushed down the riverbed of what is now the St. Croix River. Interstate Park contains 1,100 acres of woods, moss covered cliffs, and beautiful walking and riding trails.

      Location: Taylors Falls
      Hours: Daily
      Fees: Permit required. See p. 124.

Lava bluffs tower 200 feet above the St. Croix Channel. A boat ride down the Dalles of the St. Croix is a colorful and relaxing way to enjoy a summer hour. Pack a picnic lunch and explore the Interstate Park before or after your ride.

      Location: Taylors Falls
      Hours: Summer months only
      Fees: Adults ($1.50), children (75¢)
      Note: The boat tour lasts approxi-
                  mately 45 minutes.

Another way to explore the St. Croix is via a <u>paddle-your-own-canoe</u>. The setting is outstanding. At least once, consider renting a canoe and gently paddling or drifting downstream.

Location: Canoe rental organizations in Taylors Falls

Hours: Summer months

Fees: About $10/canoe provides 6-8 hours afloat. This fee includes transportation back up-river to the starting point. Straight hourly canoe rentals are also available.

Note: Bring along fishing poles, binoculars, and lunch.

The <u>William Folsom House</u> sits high above the St. Croix River. Built by a lumberman and politician, restoration of this interesting home continues.

Location: Government Road, Taylors Falls

Hours: Sunday afternoons from 2-5 pm

Fees: Adults ($1.00), children under 21 (25¢), no charge for children when accompanied by a parent

In 1964, a Pine City farmer uncovered the remains of the <u>Tom Connor Trading Post</u>. Dating back to 1804, it was one of the earliest outposts of the white man's existence in the area. Restorationwork is underway to recreate the fur trading post that once stood on the banks of the Snake River.

Location: 1-1/2 miles west of Pine City on County Road 7

Hours: May 1 through September 30 from 10 am to 6 pm. Closed on Mondays. Open weekends in October from 1-6 pm

Fees: Adults ($1.00), children (25¢), no charge for children under 16 when accompanied by a parent.

History buffs will want to visit the
Hinckley Memorial Cemetary. A simple granite
memorial marks the end of the lumbering era and
commemorates the early wilderness pioneers who
lost their lives on September 1, 1894.

In two short hours, the worst forest fire
in Minnesota's history swept through thousands
of acres of prime timberland. The blaze roared
unchecked across the land, killing many settlers,
lumberjacks, animals, and the trees. When the
smoke cleared, the remaining lumberjacks moved
further west. The era of lumbering along the
St. Croix had ended. Hinckley, the town almost
burned out by the holocaust, slowly began to
rebuild.

    Location: Rt. 18, Hinckley
    Hours: Cemetary open daily

After the fire of 1894, parts of the forest
were re-planted. The D.A.R. Forest has many
lovely lookout areas for picnics and short walks.

    Location: Rt. 23, about 20 miles northeast
               of Hinckley
    Hours: Daily
    Fees: Free

How fast would you walk across a swinging foot bridge? Come to the Jay Cooke State Park and find out! The bridge crosses the normally quiet St. Louis River. However, a visit in the Spring is particularly exciting.

> Location: Rt. 23, southwest of Duluth
> Hours: Daily
> Fees: Permit required. See p. 124.
> Note: The park is widely known for
>   its beautiful spring wildflowers
>   and autumn foliage.

Duluth's Skyline Drive begins on the out-skirts of the city. It provides a memorable first view of this international seaport.

> Location: Watch for the well marked "Sky-
>   line Drive" signs as you approach
>   the city.

The Enger Memorial Tower offers another marvelous way to see Duluth.

> Location: 18th Ave., West on the Skyline
>   Drive
> Hours: Daily
> Fees: Free
> Note: Binoculars would be helpful!

Just next to the Tower is a small pond which is often stocked to attract children's fishing poles.

> Location: North Pond, 18th Ave., West on
>   the Skyline Drive
> Hours: Daily
> Fees: Free

DULUTH

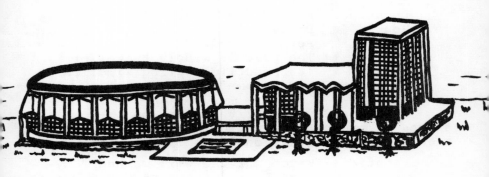

One of the first white men to visit Duluth was Daniel Greysolon, Sieur Du Luth. He came in 1679 to try to make peace between the Chippewa and Sioux Indian Tribes. This mission paved the way for the Voyageurs (see p. 11) to travel safely within Indian territory.

Duluth grew to become a city during the 1800s. It was a base camp for the copper and gold seekers who poured into the area in the mid-1800s. But, by 1873, the town was almost deserted as a gigantic financial depression reduced the city to only two inhabited dwellings. Duluth looked like a ghost town.

A decade later, the first big ore mine began sending iron ore to Duluth for shipment to the East Coast via Lake Superior. The city was reborn and serves as a link between the great mid-west (with its ore and grain) and the rest of the world.

The statue of <u>Sieur Du Luth</u> is interesting, controversial, or fascinating--depending upon which Duluthian you ask to comment upon it! Done in bronze by the world famous sculptor, Jacques Lipchitz, it is on display in the Ordean Court, University of Minnesota Campus, Duluth.

23

NE-Duluth

Park your car and climb aboard the
<u>Aerial Lift Bridge</u>. This is the largest and
fastest lift bridge in the world. It rises
138 feet in 55 seconds.

Location: Foot of Lake Avenue
Hours: Bridge rides offered during
             summer months only
Fees: Small charge

A special outing for the entire family is a visit to the U.S. Coast Guard Cutter Woodrush.

Location: 12 blocks south of the Aerial
             Bridge on the Bay Side
Hours: Open for inspection on weekends
             and holidays from 1-4 pm (when
             in port!)
Fees: Free

Excursion boats criss-cross Duluth's busy harbor during the summer months. They provide an impressive waterside way to enjoy the area.

Location: Foot of 5th Street, West
Hours: From June 1 to Labor Day. Boats
             leave every 2 hours from 9 am to
             7 pm.
Fees: Adults ($3.00), children ($1.25)
Note: Boat tour is approximately 1-3/4
             hours long.

Duluthians can tell an "Oceangoer" from a "Laker"--and they can do this from across the harbor. You, too, will be able to identify the commercial ships with the aid of an excellent, free Boatwatcher's Guide. It is available by writing to the Duluth Chamber of Commerce, or by stopping at the Convention and Visitor's Bureau Information Booth in Duluth.

Imagine seeing twelve oceangoing ships lined up at an ore dock. The Burlington Northern Observation Platform overlooks the largest ore-loading operations in the world.

Location: 36th Avenue, East at the end of
             1st Street
Hours: You know boats are being loaded
             by the clanging sound in the air.
             After you've identified it the
             first time, you'll always know
             the sound.
Fees: Free

An excellent close-up view of ore-loading can be seen at the <u>Duluth, Mesabi & Iron Range Railroad Viewpoint</u>. Although a smaller facility than the one just described, many people seem to be able to follow the activity more easily from this spot.

Location:	Foot of 35th Ave., West off Interstate Hwy. 35
Hours:	Listen for the clanging sound
Fees:	Free

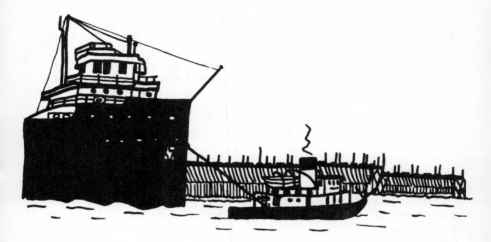

In 1926, Duluth residents stood at their harbor and watched a boat come in from Bergen, Norway. This <u>half-size replica of Leif Erikson's famous boat</u> has now been grounded and enjoys an excellent mooring in the park.

Location:	Leif Erikson Park, 12th Avenue, East and London Road
Hours:	Daily
Fees:	Free

The sky darkens for days over Duluth as the annual <u>Hawk Migration</u> takes place overhead. In 1970, over 70,000 birds flew over the city in a 24 hour period.

Location: Drive east on Superior Street to 45th Ave., East. Turn left and drive to end of 45th Ave, turn left on Summit Ave. and go to Skyline Drive which is the first road to the right. Follow Skyline Drive to the first Lookout and drive to the side for parking and viewing.

Note: Contact the Audubon Society for the best dates to watch this fascinating migration.

The **A.M. Chisholm Museum** began as a children's museum. Although many exhibits are designed for younger viewers, an adult will particularly enjoy the American history and North Shore geology displays.

Location:	1832 E. 2nd Street
Hours:	Monday through Friday, 9 am–5 pm Saturday from 9 am to noon
Fees:	Free

The twelve acre **Fairmount Park Zoo** is fun for children of all ages!

Location:	71st Ave., West and Grand Avenue
Hours:	From May through September, daily, 10 am to 8 pm; from October through April, daily, 10 am to 4 pm
Fees:	Free on Friday and from October to April. Otherwise, adults (50¢), children from 6-12 (10¢), children under 6 are free.

The **St. Louis County Historical Society** houses an extensive collection of Chippewa Indian paintings.

Location:	2228 E. Superior St.
Hours:	Monday through Friday from 10 am to 5 pm. Open the first Sunday of the month from 2:30 to 5 pm
Fees:	Free

The University of Minnesota at Duluth is an interesting place to visit. We suggest that you drive over to the 200 acre campus high on the hill overlooking Lake Superior and explore. Among the many interesting things to do and see are:

The Tweed Museum of Art. This modern gallery houses an absorbing collection of French and American art.

Location: 26th Ave., E. and 7th St.
Hours: Tuesday through Friday from 10 am to 5 pm. Saturday and Sunday afternoons. Closed Monday
Fees: Free

The Alworth Planetarium. Take time to visit the stars!

Location: On the University Campus
Hours: October to May on Thursdays at 7:30 pm, Sundays at 2:30 pm
Fees: Free

The Duluth Playhouse is the oldest community theatre in America which is still in existence. Besides a full season program, the Playhouse sponsors a popular Children's Theatre and a summer Shakespeare in the Parks Program.

Location: 6 S. 12th Avenue, East
Note: Watch the Duluth newspaper or phone the Playhouse for program details and ticket reservations.

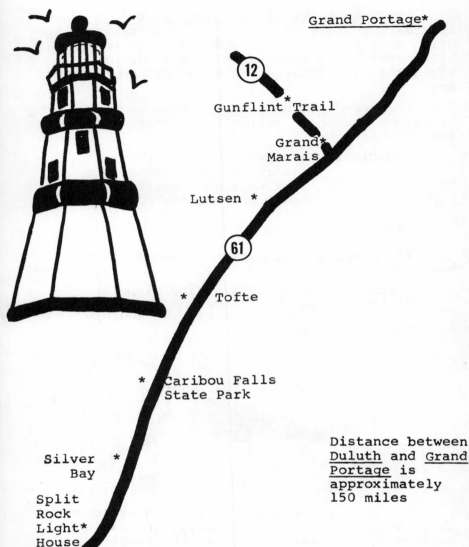

Grand Portage*

12

Gunflint *Trail

Grand*
Marais

Lutsen *

61

* Tofte

* Caribou Falls
State Park

Distance between
<u>Duluth</u> and <u>Grand</u>
<u>Portage</u> is
approximately
150 miles

Silver *
Bay

Split
Rock
Light*
House

* Gooseberry
Falls State Park

* Two Harbors

* French River

*<u>Duluth</u>

Breathtaking scenery is highlighted by jagged cliffs, swift streams, and tumbling waterfalls. The everchanging moods of Lake Superior await your travels along the magnificent North Shore Drive.

The <u>French River Fish Hatchery</u>'s freshwater fish pools are interesting to visit. As these fish grow, they will be transported to northern Minnesota's streams--and your fishing line?

        Location: French River
        Hours: Daily during the summer months
        Fees: Free

The <u>Lake County Historical Society Museum</u> contains interesting exhibits relating to the area's early mining days. Guarding the museum is the Three Spot (the first locomotive to carry ore between the Tower-Soudan Mine and Two Harbors).

        Location: Two Harbors, 8 blocks south of
                    Highway 61 at the ore loading
                    docks.
        Hours: June 1 to September 30 from
                    9 am to 4 pm, Monday through
                    Saturday; 1 to 4 pm on Sunday.
        Fees: Free

<u>Chalcedonies</u> litter the North Shore Beaches. Harder than steel (but more brittle), these translucent stones were once known for their magical powers. The chalcedonies (or <u>agates</u>) found along the shores of Lake Superior are often polished and used for bracelets, cuff links, and rings. As you rock hunt, look for variegated stones through which you can see light (when the stone is held up to the sky). These are agates. We usually combine a rock hunt with a picnic lunch and finger-dip into Lake Superior where the water is <u>always</u> cold.

The Gooseberry River cascades over three thirty-foot waterfalls within <u>Gooseberry Falls State Park</u>.

        Location: North of Two Harbors on Hwy. 61
        Hours: Daily
        Fees: Permit required. See p. 124.

A new era began for the <u>Split Rock Light-house</u> on May 1, 1971 when the brilliant light again swept Lake Superior's waters. The light-house was built in 1909. At that time there was no road along the lake and the building site could be reached only by water. And so, tons of brick, cement, metal and lumber were hauled off the boats and up the 170 foot vertical cliff. It was a tremendous task. The Federal Government had the light built to warn boats away from the treacherous cliffs and dangerous rocks in the area. Heavy ore deposits in the rocks made compass navigation unreliable and many boats went down before the light was built. Some people suggest that the North Shore offers the tourist a touch of New England and the rocky coast of Maine. However, in 1971 most of the Maine coast is filled with tourist lodges and drive-in theatres and amusement parks. The deer and bear and birds have left the coastland. Come to Minnesota's North Shore to see how Maine's North Shore used to be!

        Location: North of Two Harbors on
                     Hwy. 61
        Hours: Daily
        Fees: Permit required. See p. 124.

Days Hill Trail begins at the Split Rock Wayside Area and emerges high above Lake Superior. Bring binoculars and something to eat as you look way, way down past the Lighthouse and out over the lake.

Location: Split Rock Wayside Area
Hours: Daily
Fees: Permit required. See p. 124.

Silver Bay was little more than a bus stop in 1955 when Reserve Mining began to build housing for the employees at their Taconite Plant. More than 6,000 people live in "new" Silver Bay.

Tour a taconite pellet plant. Reserve Mining's Silver Bay Plant can process 10.7 million tons of taconite a year.

Location: Silver Bay
Hours: Tours given by appointment only on Monday through Friday during the summer months.
Fees: Free
Note: Tours limited to persons over 16. No cameras are permitted within the plant area. Ladies are required to wear slacks and low heeled shoes.

While in Silver Bay, stop at the Ore Docks Viewpoint. The entire family enjoys watching the dock loading equipment.

Location: A short distance southeast of Hwy. 61 opposite Silver Bay's business district.
Hours: Listen for the clanging sound in the air which signifies that loading operations are in progress.
Fees: Free
Note: Attendants are often on duty to answer your questions, provide rock samples, and offer descriptive literature.

Don't pass <u>Caribou Falls State Park</u> without stopping to watch the Caribou River shoot over the cliffs in a breathtaking cascade of water. The waterfall is an easy half-mile walk up the trail.

Location:	North of Silver Bay on Hwy. 61
Hours:	Daily
Fees:	Permit required. See p. 124.

Watch Mama Bear and her cubs enjoy a gourmet dinner at the <u>Tofte Bear Pit</u>, but be sure to stay in your car!

Location:	Tofte
Hours:	Late afternoon and early evening
Fees:	Free

Minnesota's wilderness is beginning. Big game hunting, superlative fishing, clean air camping, canoeing, and unexcelled privacy are among the reasons vacationers continue North.

The Gunflint Trail winds north from Grand Marais via Rt. 12 to "the end of the road." This is an exceptionally interesting route to follow. For, besides beautiful forest and lake country, there are numerous areas for hiking and camping. A few of our favorites are:

Eagle Mountain Trail - Eagle Mountain is the highest point in Minnesota (2,301 feet above sea level.

Magnetic Rock Trail - Hike to the 40 foot high vertical slab of rock. Its magnetism makes compass naviagion unreliable. Geologists believe the rock formation was set down as the wildly rushing waters of the melting glaciers sped through the state.

Twenty-five miles west of Grand Portage (see p. 14), set like a jewel above Lake Superior's sparkling waters, is Isle Royale National Park. This rugged, wilderness island has no cars, no roads. The wildlife is exceptional (including a resident herd of moose and fox): So are the wild flowers. If your family enjoys an outdoor vacation, we recommend the Greenstone Ridge Trail. This 45 mile trail leads the hiker along the rugged island's coastline. There are lodges at either end of the trail, but the middle is just for hikers and campers.

Location:	Excursion boats leave from the Grand Portage dock
Hours:	Summer months only
Note:	All hikers and campers are required to check-in at the ranger's station on the island before beginning extensive hikes. This is for your protection. Please comply with the regulation.

Distance between <u>Duluth</u>
and <u>Tower Soudan</u> is
approximately 85 miles.

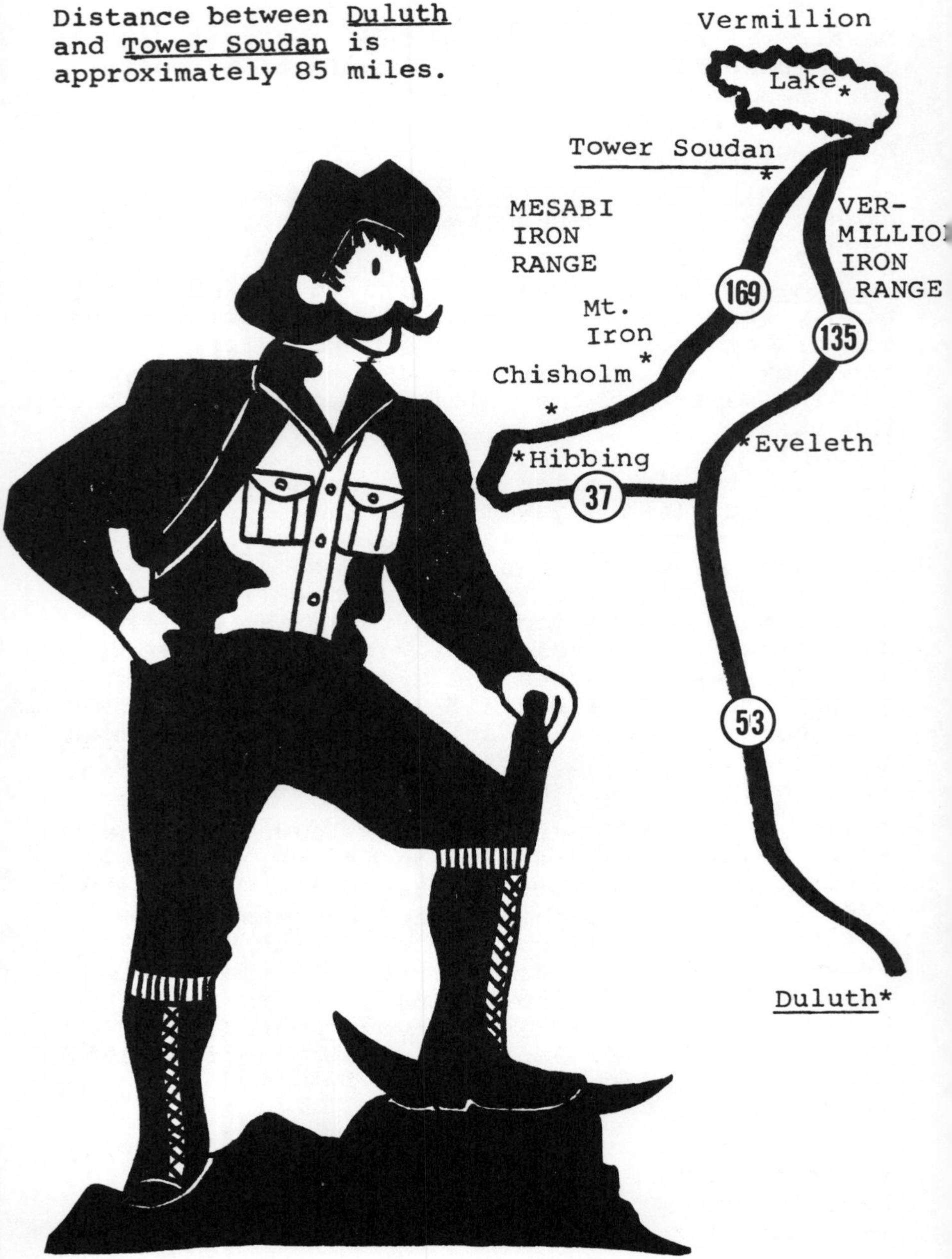

Vermillion

Lake *

Tower Soudan
*

MESABI
IRON
RANGE

VER-
MILLIO
IRON
RANGE

(169)

(135)

Mt.
Iron
Chisholm *

*

*Eveleth

*Hibbing

(37)

(53)

<u>Duluth</u>*

THE
MINER'S
TRAIL

In 1865, geologists announced that *GOLD* had been found on the shores of Lake Vermillion. The Minnesota Gold Rush was on! Miners poured into the state from around the world and began prospecting in the area.

Lewis Merritt and George Stuntz were among the many fortune hunters "working" Vermillion's shores. Months passed, but they found no ore. However, working independently and at different locations, both men found a dark, reddish substance and remembered it.

Merritt finally admitted defeat. He picked up his gear and headed back to Missouri. As his seven little boys were growing up, they often heard stories of the rich ore deposit. The seven Merritt men spent more than 20 years combining their lumbering jobs with the continuing search for ore. Finally, in 1890, their employee, J. A. Nichols, made the find. They named the ore and the location "Mountain Iron." They began to work their claim. Hematite, as the ore was to be named, was much softer than any ore previously mined. It created many problems for the steelmakers who questioned its potential.

The Merritts realized it would be necessary to transport the ore to Duluth. They became heavily committed to building a railroad and were soon financially overextended.

At this bleak moment, more than 25 years after their father had first discovered the ore deposit, at a time when many had lost hope that hematite could be successfully made into steel, John D. Rockefeller bought out the almost bankrupt Merritt brothers.

Rockefeller invested wisely. He spent vast sums to make the Mesabi (an Indian word for "giant") Range productive. He helped steelmakers learn how to process hematite and, with his marketing genius, made financial history in Northern Minnesota.

A short distance from the spot that was to become Mountain Iron, George Stuntz also admitted defeat as a gold miner. He thought about the rich ore deposit he had found and contacted a Philadelphia investor. Jay Cooke came west.

Cooke and Stuntz decided their first move should be to build a railroad from Lake Vermillion to Duluth. Here, as with the Merritt operation, the expenses involved had not been adequately estimated. Manpower was costly. The winter was long and severe. The forests were difficult to work through. However, these obstacles might have been surmounted had it not been for the Great Financial Depression of 1873.

The Depression hit hard and fast. Banks closed, people panicked, entire towns were deserted as "townsfolk" returned to a safer existence on the farms. Cooke and Stuntz abandoned their project.

A short time later, a wealthy Pennsylvanian sent agents into the area to buy land for him. Charlemagne Tower soon owned over 20,000 acres of prime mining land. He had not paid much for it. Mr. Tower knew the value of his investment and he began to develop what would become the Tower-Soudan Mine.

Serious mining began in 1884. It continues today with taconite replacing hematite as the prime ore being removed from mines and pits. Millions and millions of dollars worth of ore

have been removed from the gently rolling hillsides.
We are fortunate to be able to explore the Miner's
Trail today. Although the machinery and methods
are more sophisticated, the area still retains
the feeling of a world where Louis Merritt and
George Stuntz panned for gold, but found iron
ore.

The Tower Soudan Mine is an adventurer's
delight. Combine a 2,400 foot elevator ride, a
train ride through a long tunnel, and a mining
museum far underground and you will begin to
understand the fun involved in a visit into the
mine. Tower Soudan was the first underground
mining operation in Minnesota. Opened in 1884,
vast quantities of ore were brought to the surface before U.S. Steel closed the mine and
donated it and 1,000 surrounding acres to the
State. The entire family will remember this
visit toward the center of the earth.

Location: 1/2 mile north of Soudan, 2
           miles northeast of Tower on
           Hwy. 169
Hours: From the 3rd week in May through
           the first week in September.
           Open for tours from 11 am to 4 pm
Fees: Admission charged
Note: Bring a sweater. The temperature
           within the mine is a cool 52°.

Hibbing has a fascinating history. "Old"
Hibbing was a rough mining town until 1922 when
a rich ore deposit was discovered directly
beneath the main street. In no time at all,
"Old" Hibbing was leveled, mining began, and
"New" Hibbing emerged as a clean, relatively
quiet, modern community.

The Hull-Rust-Mahoning Mine marks the site
of "Old" Hibbing. Called the "Grand Canyon of
the West" and the "biggest man-made hole in the
world," Hull-Rust-Mahoning's observation viewpoint permits the visitor a mammoth look at
open pit mining.

Location: 1-1/2 mile north of Hibbing on
Howard St. to 1st Ave., E., to
17th St. to 3rd Ave., E. Viewpoint is on the left.

Hours: June 1 to Labor Day from 9 am to
9 pm, Monday through Saturday

Fees: Free

While in Hibbing it is fun to recall that
the giant Greyhound Bus empire had its beginning
as a 15¢ ride between Hibbing and Alice, Minn.

The Viewpoint in the Sky is 20 stories
above the deepest part of an open mine. Look
down and gasp.

Location: 1-1/2 mile east of Virginia,
1/2 mile off Hwy. 169.

Hours: Attendants at the site from
July 1 through Labor Day.
Open Monday through Saturday
from 8 am to 5 pm.

Fees: Free

Note: Bring the binoculars.

The Sherman Mine Viewpoint offers a grand
look at ore trains and electric shovels.

Location: 1 mile east of Chisholm, Hwy. 169

Hours: Monday through Saturday, 8 am to
5 pm, July 1 through Labor Day

Fees: Free

The **Minnesota Museum of Mining** is a huge fortress-like building. It houses a wide variety of mining implements and the guides do an excellent job of bringing the mining days to life. Surrounding the Museum is a reconstructed mine and 13 acres of mining exhibits. Be sure to see the ore trucks, steam shovel, and an early locomotive.

Location: West Lake St., Chisholm, at the junction of Rts. 169 and 73

Hours: May 30 to Labor Day from 9 am to 6 pm

Fees: Admission charged for tour

Note: Tours are conducted every hour on the hour and last about 45 minutes.

U.S. Steel provides an interesting tour through their recently completed **Minnetac Plant**—a taconite processing facility.

Location: Mt. Iron Recreation Bldg., 2nd Ave. off Hwy. 169

Hours: July 1 through Labor Day from 8:30 am to 4:30 pm

Fees: Free

Note: Tours last approximately 90 minutes. Free tour busses provided.

For more mining-related activities, visit the ore-loading docks along the shore of Lake Superior (see p. 25) and examine the North Shore Drive section of this book (see p. 31).

NORTHWESTERN
MINNESOTA

"This is America--a town of a few thousand, in a region of wheat and corn and dairies and little groves." So wrote Sinclair Lewis of his hometown, Sauk Centre. However, his comments pertain to the entire northwestern region. This is an area of rural communities which are primarily farm related, located upon some of the world's richest agricultural soil. It is an area of prosperous trade with few industrial centers spread over gently rolling, cultivated countryside.

The central section is, indeed, a land of lakes. Pure, fresh air mingles with the scent of pine, superlative views, biting fish, and all the conveniences of an expanding resort business to make it "easy" to come exploring.

The following tours cover northwestern Minnesota's development from the glacial age to the present.

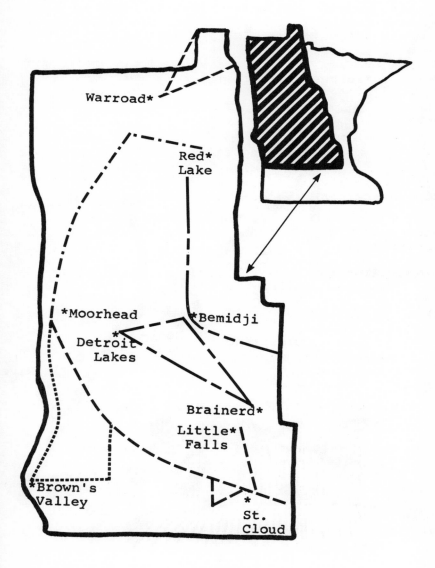

NORTHWESTERN
MINNESOTA

Warroad*

Red*
Lake

*Moorhead   *Bemidji

Detroit*
Lakes

Brainerd*

Little*
Falls

*Brown's
Valley

*
St.
Cloud

43

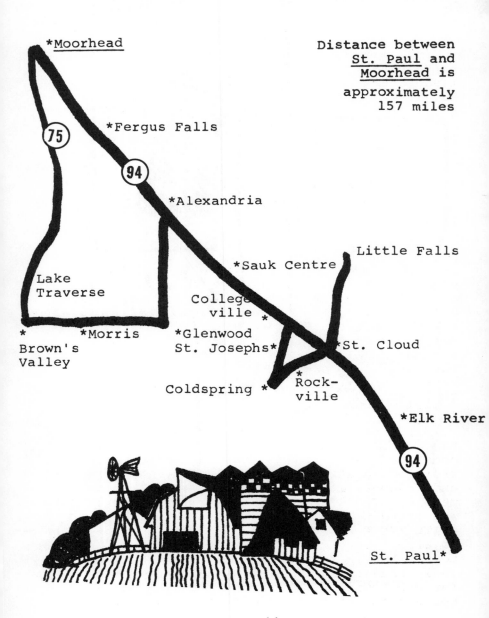

*Moorhead

Distance between
St. Paul and
Moorhead is
approximately
157 miles

(75)

*Fergus Falls

(94)

*Alexandria

Little Falls

*Sauk Centre

College
ville
*

Lake
Traverse

*   *Morris   *Glenwood
Brown's   St. Josephs*   *St. Cloud
Valley

                                              *
Coldspring *   Rock-
                              ville

*Elk River

(94)

St. Paul*

44

Little more than a hundred years ago, a dusty,
rutted trail wound from St. Paul, through the
Minnesota territory, and into North Dakota. The
Red River Oxcarts originally carried fur pelts,
but in the 1850s and '60s, long trains of
oxcarts carried settlers into the middle west.
These brave pioneers, often immigrants newly
arrived from Europe, streamed west to acquire
land under the homesteading acts. They travelled
inland to St. Paul where wagon train outfitters
helped the families purchase seed and basic
supplies in preparation for the momentous over-
land journey to the land that would be home.

One route led from St. Paul, through St.
Cloud and on toward Moorhead and the Dakota
border. The oxcarts were primitive. The early
vehicles did have wheels, but they were formed
of solid oak. St. Cloud residents used to insist that they could hear a wagon train coming
for days before it finally arrived. The
cacophony of sound as wooden wheels scraped
against metal fittings, the endless bumping as
the oxcarts jogged along the rutted roads may
have contributed to the numbers of families
that decided to make their new home in the
fertile Red River Valley area.

The settlers applied for the Government
Land Grants. They began to farm and build
homes and later schools and communities. Aside
from Indian attack, tornado, grasshopper plague,
and drought, life was fairly easy for these
people. The land was good. They and their sons
and grandsons appreciated the soil and used it
well. Today's three and four siloed farms stand
as a testimony to the pioneer's tenacious ability
to survive in the face of overwhelming odds.
Their bravery made life in a wilderness easier
for succeeding generations. Today's farmland
represents the best of a giant industry.

Distance between
<u>Elk River</u> and
<u>Sauk Centre</u> is
approximately
120 miles.

*<u>Little Falls</u>
  (about 33 miles to
   St. Cloud)

*<u>Sauk</u>
 <u>Centre</u>

Collegeville*
  St. Joseph*   *St. Cloud

(10)

(2) (23)

*Rockville

Cold*
Spring

(94)

Elk River*

Twin Cities*
(approx. 15
miles south)

Pack a picnic lunch, get into the car, and spend a summer day learning about three of Minnesota's great men, exploring an exciting college campus, and remembering a bit of the early settler's world.

Oliver Kelley revolutionized the farmer's world. Within the kitchen of his now restored homestead, he planned the organization that was to become the National Grange. Kelley longed "to see the great army of producers in our country, turn their eyes up from their work;... let them feel that they are human beings and the strength of the nation,...and farming the highest calling on earth."

Location: 2 miles south of Elk River on Hwy. 10 and 169
Hours: May 1 to October 1 from 10 am to 4 pm (closed Mondays). Open weekends in October from 1-4 pm
Fees: Adults ($1.00), children (25¢), children under 16 accompanied by a parent (free)

ST. CLOUD

The first granite quarry in Minnesota was opened in 1868 on the site of what is now the St. Cloud Reformatory. Of interest is the fact that the wall around the reformatory is the largest granite wall in the country.

Location: Rt. 10, just east of St. Cloud

St. Cloud began as three small towns on the Mississippi River. In the early 1800s, these settlements made convenient way stations for

47

west-ward bound settlers. One of the towns was
established by S.B. Lowry, a politician and
trader. It was primarily settled by slave-hold-
ing Southerners. The second town was established
by J.L. Wilson, a saw miller, storekeeper, and
legislator. His town was primarily settled by
Catholic immigrants from Germany. The third
town was established by G.F. Brott, a professional
promotor. His town was occupied by anti-
slavery Protestants. It's easy to imagine the
friction that probably existed between these three
"neighborly" communities!

Finally, in 1856, the 3 settlements combined
under the name of St. Cloud. (The glamour of
likening what was then a wilderness tri-post to
Napoleon's famous French residence must have been
a compromise decision!) With merger came a
greater degree of town unity. When colored
granite deposits were found in 1868, the area's
economic destiny was assured.

Modern St. Cloud is filled with superior
schools and colleges, handsome mansions, a
healthy granite industry, and a thriving business
community. Pause and explore a city with an
unusual past and a dynamic present.

St. Cloud State College is beautifully
situated on a bend in the Mississippi River.
Started with 53 students in 1869, the college
is now the second largest of Minnesota's state
colleges with an enrollment near 10,000. Of
particular interest is the performing arts
complex.

Location: State College is roughly bounded
             by 3rd and 10th Streets, 3rd
             Avenue and the Mississippi
Hours: Daily
Note: Tours arranged upon advance
             request.

Munsinger Gardens are beautiful during the summer months. Pause to enjoy the bubbling fountains, multihued flowers, and restful setting.

    Location: Riverside Park at Riverside Drive
    Hours: Daily
    Fees: Free

The Sterns County Historical Society has an intriguing collection of historical artifacts.

    Location: 4th Avenue and Highway 23

LITTLE FALLS

Just 33 miles north of St. Cloud is the home of Charles A. Lindbergh, one of Minnesota's foremost political leaders. His son, Charles, Jr., lived on the farm as a boy and recalled, "The old farm at Little Falls is the only other place I have loved as much." The farmhouse has been restored to the way it looked in the early 1900s when young Charles played here. A new Interpretive Center is under construction which will feature the lives of three generations of Lindberghs and will include details from that fantastic flight, solo and non-stop, from New York to Paris in 1927 that electrified the world. "Lone Eagle," Charles A. Lindbergh, Jr. is a legend in his own time. Come to his boyhood world.

    Location: 2 miles south of Little Falls on the west side of the Mississippi River, Lindbergh Drive and County Rd. 52.
    Hours: Mid-April through October, closed Mondays. Otherwise, open from 10 am to 5 pm (June, July, August), Sundays 10 am - 6 pm. 10 am to 4 pm (April, May, September, October), Sundays 1 - 4.
    Fees: Free

ROCKVILLE

Bring binoculars to see what may be the largest <u>Blue Heron Rookery</u> in America. The 1970 survey showed 900 nests in the area. The great blue heron is a mighty bird, often weighing up to 70 pounds.

Location: Rt. 23, 3-1/2 miles south of Rockville, 1/2 mile north of Cold Spring. Watch for the nests high in the trees on the right side of the road (if you pass Jim's Auto Body Shop on the left, you've gone too far!).

Hours: Spring and summer

Fees: Free to watch FROM YOUR CAR.

Note: The Rookery is on private property. Please be content to watch from the roadside. Do not spoil this exceptional sight for people yet to come by trying to get close and frightening the birds away.

COLD SPRING

The <u>Grasshopper Chapel</u> serves as a reminder of the early farmer's tremendous struggle for survival. Around June 14, 1873, swarms of grasshoppers jumped into farming villages. A light harvest was gathered that fall, but conditions grew worse each year. By 1877, there was not a green leaf to be seen. The people were ready to give up, to leave the farms they had worked so hard to start. One story comes from a town further south. The grasshoppers came in clouds so thick they hid the sun, they were piled up to a depth of 1 to 2 feet and horses could hardly be driven through them. Railroad trains were blockaded until the tracks were cleared. This was the prairie farmer's plight in 1877. Then, unaccountably, the grasshoppers simply hopped on, never to become a serious threat again.

The townspeople near Cold Spring built a small chapel to thank God and in hopes of

averting another plague. In 1894, the chapel
was destroyed by a tornado. It was rebuilt in
1951.

    Location: Rt. 23, just northeast of Cold
                  Spring
    Hours: Daily
    Fees: Free

ST. JOSEPH

We move gently back to the 20th century
with a visit to a nunnery and small liberal arts
college, St. Benedict. Be sure to see the
exquisite Benedicta Arts Center. There is an
art gallery in the west lobby with first-rate
exhibits. The acoustics within the music hall
are superb.

    Location: College Avenue South,
    Hours: Daily
    Fees: Tours of the college can be
                  arranged upon advance request,
                  at no charge.

COLLEGEVILLE

Set on the side of a lake in a heavily
wooded glen is the largest Benedictine monestary
in the world. The major work of the St. John's
Community is the staffing of the various schools
at the College. For the Benedictine professors,
this is home, life and vocation. The men are
dedicated to teaching, the students respond.
The Benedictine community at St. John's states
that theirs is a lifetime of freedom, of friend-
ship, and of service to others.

The monestary is impressive, as is the old
church. However, in the late 1950s, Marcel
Breuer was commissioned to create a new house of
worship for St. John's. The Abbey Church was
his creation. It was dedicated in 1961 and is
considered by many to be the most striking piece
of architecture in Minnesota.

We urge you to visit the Campus of St. John's University and to attend a service at the Abbey Church. It is an experience which will be yours to remember for years to come.

Each element of the church has a symbolic reason for being. The dramatic bell banner is strikingly modern, yet recalls the early mission architecture of southwestern America. The banner serves as a proclamation. It announces the church. However, it also provides a feeling to those who step under the great parabolic arch that this is a building which is not to be entered into lightly. This is indeed a church where a feeling of reverence steps out to greet you.

Once beyond the entrance, note the Baptismal Font, recessed into the floor. You descend 3 steps to be blessed and rise cleansed of your sins on the other side.

Then, into the sanctuary. Spacious, soaring
walls, all leading the eye to the altar. It is
only later that one becomes aware of the magnifi-
cence of the wall of stained glass windows.

No superlatives are elaborate enough. Attend
Mass at the Abbey Church--no matter what your
religion. And take the children. This is a
special, special place.

Throughout the Church there is beautiful
art. The Holtkamp Organ, with over 3,000 pipes,
is outstanding. We are grateful to the
Benedictines for sharing this contemporary
church which is firmly rooted in the best of
centuries of church architecture.

Location: On the Campus of St. John's
            University, Collegeville
Hours: The Abbey Church is always open.
            Masses are held at least several
            times daily. Ask at the College
            Information Center at the build-
            ing to the right of the church
            for the current schedule.
Fees: No charge
Note: Marcel Breuer is still at work
            on the St. John's Campus. Take
            a leisurely walk and see if you
            can identify his other buildings.

Sinclair Lewis was a gauky, sensitive child. He had little success in school and was unmercifully teased by his classmates. Born in 1865, he grew up in Sauk Centre, a raw prairie town only 5 or 6 blocks long. "Red" spent his boyhood tagging after his older brother and his father, who was the town's doctor. He graduated from Yale in 1908. Although he had been writing since he was 15, it was with <u>Main Street</u> and <u>Babbitt</u> that he became famous as a novelist and critic of American culture. He was awarded the Nobel Prize for Literature in 1930. Lewis came back to Sauk Centre in 1931 and said of his boyhood town,

> "It was a good time and a good place and a good preparation for life."

Drive to Sauk Centre, see the "Original Main Street" and perhaps even read <u>Main Street</u> before your visit. How much change has there been in 40 years?

Much of Sinclair Lewis remains here. His home is now a museum through which guided tours are conducted.

Location: 812 Sinclair Lewis Avenue,
               Sauk Centre

Hours: Summer months. Saturdays from
               10 am-4 pm; Sundays from
               1-5 pm.

Fees: Adults ($1.00), high school
               students (50¢), children (25¢).
               There is no charge for children
               when accompanied by their
               parents.

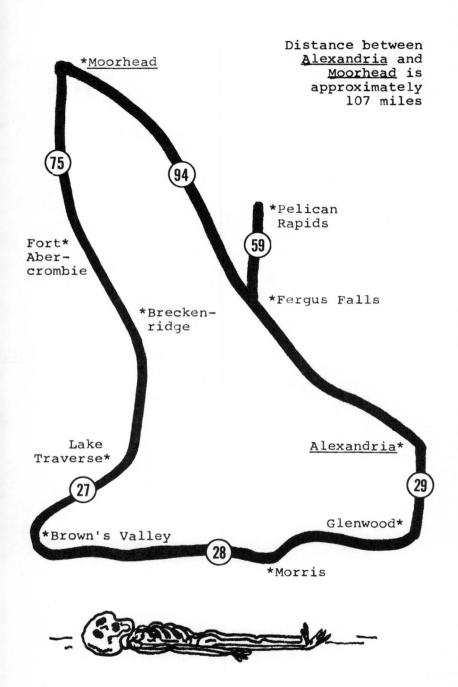

Distance between
Alexandria and
Moorhead is
approximately
107 miles

*<u>Moorhead</u>

75

94

*Pelican
Rapids

59

Fort*
Aber-
crombie

*Fergus Falls

*Brecken-
ridge

Lake
Traverse*

<u>Alexandria</u>*

27

29

Glenwood*

*Brown's Valley

28

*Morris

Minnesota has not yet become a prime archaeological investigative location. We expect this will change within the next decade. Two of the oldest skeletons on the North American continent have been found within about 100 miles of Moorhead. In addition, there is some evidence to suggest that an inland visit to America by Vikings predated Columbus' much heralded trip.

Within recorded history, April 19 stands out as a day for great patriots. In 1776, Paul Revere undertook his stirring ride to warn that the British were coming. On April 19, 1866, Sam Brown travelled 120 miles through a lashing storm to warn settlers that the Dakota Sioux were planning an attack.

This is one of the state's richest areas. A trip along this route is always a special pleasure for children. First, they see Vikings and Indians and settlers and Cavalry officers at every bend. They become captivated by the thought of prehistoric skeletons which have been found just a few feet from the surface. After some imaginary digging for relics, it is fun to lazily picnic along the shores of the Red River. The pace picks up as the children become members of the 1857 U.S. Army Post guarding settlers from an Indian attack. The day goes on and on this way. The trip is fun, informative, and the scenery is beautiful.

The Kensington Runestone is a controversial part of Minnesota's history. In 1898, a farmer discovered a strange tablet in his field. Carved in Runic characters, it told the story of how 8 Goths and 22 Norwegians travelled from Vinland into Minnesota--in 1362. (A similar tablet has been found in Iowa.)

The Runestone is presently being studied at the Smithsonian Institute. Believers in its authenticity contend that the interior of Minnesota was once partially flooded and a direct waterway existed from the Hudson Bay, along the Red River, and across land now dry. Mooring stones (rocks with deep, narrow holes) to which the Vikings may have anchored their ships, have been found. Some say that Big Lake Cormorant is the site of the massacres described on the stone.

Location:	The Runestone Museum at the foot of Broadway in Alexandria
Hours:	Summer months from 9 am to 9 pm.
Fees:	Adults ($1.00), less for children.
Note:	The kids will enjoy looking at the reproduction of a Viking Ship which is moored in the Museum's parking area.

Three miles north of Pelican Rapids is the
Minnesota Man (or, if you prefer, "Lady of the
Lakes") Site. In 1931, a skeleton was found by
a highway crew. One crew member noticed something white as the earth moving equipment bit
into the ground. Work was stopped. The state
archaeologist was called. Professor A.E. Jenks
carefully examined the skeleton. Some say the
teenaged girl's skeleton dates back to the
Glacial Age--at least 11,000 years ago. Others
contend that the skeleton only dates back to
"early prehistoric times." However, should the
11,000 year old figure stand, the Minnesota Man
may well be the oldest skeleton yet unearthen
on this continent. WE ADVISE YOU THAT THE
SKELETON IS NOT ON THE SITE. The location is
well marked and interesting to explore.

Location: 3 miles north of Pelican Rapids
             on Hwy.
Hours: Daily
Fees: Free

As you drive through Moorhead, the largest
city on Minnesota's western border, it should be
noted that the Red River of the North forms the
boundary between Moorhead and Fargo, North
Dakota. The Red River is one of the few rivers
in America which flows north--with its outlet
in Lake Winnipeg, Canada. Although the river is
545 miles long, its mouth is only 270 miles from
the source. As you drive along the border, you
will appreciate how much the Red River winds and
meanders along its way.

Sugar beet farming is a big industry in the
Red River Valley. One of the most interesting
plant tours in Moorhead is a visit to the
American Crystal Sugar Company.

Location: North 11th Street, Moorhead
Hours: Tours are given by appointment
             only from mid-October to
             January
Fees: Free

NW-Moorhead, Ft. Abercrombie, N.D.

You can see a 15th century battle-ax, Civil War mementos, and many relics of the pioneering days at the Clay County Historical Society Museum.

    Location: 807 North 11 Street
    Hours: Monday through Friday from
                  2 to 5 pm
    Fees: Free

The Concordia College Choir is world famous. Perhaps your visit will coincide with one of their on-campus performances.

    Location: About 8 blocks south of Moorhead
                  on Hwy. 75
    Hours: Daily
    Fees: Admission charged for some
                  concerts
    Note: Campus tours provided. Please
                  make advance arrangements by
                  writing or phoning the college.

Fort Abercrombie, North Dakota is a beautifully reconstructed reminder of one aspect of the wilderness past. In 1857, U.S. Army men arrived on the brink of the frontier. They set up the Fort to provide some degree of protection to the arriving settlers. Fort Abercrombie withstood the Indian attacks in 1862 and, when the new nation's events had made it obsolete, was abandoned in 1877.

    Location: Hwy. 75 south of Moorhead.
                  Turn right onto Co. Rd. 1 for
                  1 mile to the Fort (just over
                  the Red River).
    Hours: Daily
    Fees: Free
    Note: As you approach the Fort, watch
                  for the 5 foot high-water
                  mark (a sign on a tree on the
                  right side of the road) dating
                  from 1897.

Breckenridge serves to punctuate Fort Abercrombie's importance. In 1862, the town's citizens were warned of an impending Indian attack. All but three townspeople fled to the protection of the Fort. The three men who remained behind were massacred. Breckenridge became a ghost town and remained one until the railroad reached the area in 1871. It has been growing steadily for the past hundred years!

Location: Just off Hwy. 75

Wheaton marks the beginning of a leisurely, winding drive along the banks of the Red River.

Location: Hwy. 127 southwest from Wheaton, continue on Hwy. 27 to Lake Traverse and Brown's Valley.

Although the species is almost unknown east of the Mississippi, a tremendous flock of **Blue Geese** visit **Lake Traverse** annually. They rest here during the migration between the Gulf of Mexico and the Arctic Circle. Look for these large birds with white heads, dark bodies, and pink feet.

Location: Lake Traverse, Rt. 27
Note: Phone your local Audubon Society for specific migration dates. They vary slightly from year to year.

The **Brown's Valley Man** has disappeared!
In 1895, a village school teacher noticed some flaked quartz fragments near what is now Brown's Valley. He realized that the area might once have been the location of a post-glacial, prehistoric culture and told friends and students of his conviction.

Thirty-eight years later, W. H. Jurson, a local amateur archaeologist, found a skeleton. It was examined at the University of Minnesota, said to be at least 8,000 years old, and returned to Mr. Jurson. Imagine the excitement in the area! We imagine that everyone in town spent at least a few hours digging for that prehistoric culture--we certainly would have!

In any case, between then and now, something has become of the Brown's Valley Man. No one knows, or tells, where that skeleton is. But, some do say that on dark, moonlit nights....

Location: Site marker about 1/2 mile from the town on Hwy. 27.

The West Central Agricultural Experimental Station, the University of Minnesota at Morris, and the United States Department of Agriculture Field Station offer tours of their facilities. These three institutions are dedicated to the advancement of agriculture. It is appropriate that they be located in an area where 96% of the county's land is farmed.

Location: Near Morris
Hours: Weekdays. Tours are available by advance reservation.
Fees: Free

If Dad is a fisherman, he will thoroughly enjoy a visit to the Glenwood Fish Hatchery Pools. Just watch his angling arm twitch as he anticipates catching these trout after they have grown and grown and GROWN.

Location: Glenwood
Hours: Outdoor pools open daily
Fees: Free

Distance between <u>Moorhead</u> and <u>Agassiz</u> is approximately 130 miles.

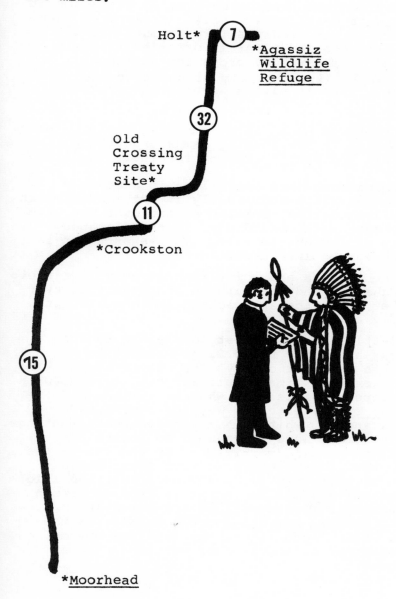

Holt* (7) *<u>Agassiz Wildlife Refuge</u>

(32)

Old Crossing Treaty Site*

(11)

*Crookston

(15)

*<u>Moorhead</u>

The flat prairie country north of Moorhead makes it difficult to realize that this was once the bed of a glacial lake. Lake Agassiz was larger than all the Great Lakes combined. It has provided the present day valley with some of Minnesota's most fertile soil. In an area that was once so wet, today's farmers must bring water from the Red River in order to irrigate the land. The Valley crops include wheat, beets, and a large variety of short-season produce. This is also a significant dairying center.

Crookston began as a lumbering center. Many men working in the logging camps understood the rich soil and sent to Europe for their families.

Imagine you are travelling in a covered wagon or oxcart. Your family is but a small part of the long caravan rolling up and over the wave of the next hill. Suddenly, in the distance, a group of Indians is seen. The wagon train is hastily formed into a circle.

The Indians are sometimes friendly. Trinkets are exchanged and the caravan proceeds. However, at other times the approaching Indians are not friendly and attack.

Settlers heading west complained to the Congress and urged the U.S. government to negotiate a "right of way" for the caravans. In 1863, Alexander Ramsey left St. Paul to meet with the Chippewa chiefs. At what is now the Old Crossing Treaty Site and Wayside over 1,600 Indians and 280 white men attended treaty meetings. These sessions were punctuated by feasts, horse races, and general merriment. By the end of the talks, the Indians had sold much more than a "right of way" across their land. They had sold approximately 3 million acres of land in return for financial considerations and reservation lands. This treaty changed the destiny of the middle west. Soon after, the land was opened for homesteading and pioneer settlement began in ernest.

The U.S. Government was eager to have the
land settled.   Up to 160 acres of land was given,
free, to any settler agreeing to farm the land
and work the soil for a minimum of 5 years.
Homesteading phamphlets were distributed throughout the East.   They were also printed in foreign
languages and sent throughout Europe so people
of widely differing heritages could consider
life in America.   At times, entire European towns
loaded all their possessions aboard "immigrant
boats" and came to America, their land of opportunity.

The <u>Agassiz National Wildlife Refuge</u> is
13,000 acres of moist land.   It is a marvelous
place to view bird migrations.

Location: 11 miles east of Holt via Hwy. 7
Hours: Daily
Fees: Free

THE
NORTHWEST

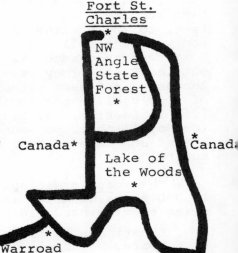

Fort St.
Charles
*
NW
Angle
State
Forest
*

Canada*

Canada

Lake of
the Woods
*

Distance between <u>Holt</u> and
<u>Warroad</u> is approximately
70 miles. We recommend
a chartered boat or plane
for the trip from <u>Warroad</u>
to <u>Fort St. Charles.</u>
Auto transportation is
possible through Canada,
but should be attempted
<u>only in dry weather.</u>

⑪
*
<u>Warroad</u>

㉜

<u>Holt</u>
*

The <u>Northwest Angle</u> is a beautiful
section with thousands of wooded
islands, a maze of coastline, and
a wealth of history. The area was
Indian territory, then came the
fur traders and their outposts,
and then Canadian settlers heading
south to the Red River Valley.
Each group has contributed to the
present area.

If you are planning a visit, we
highly recommend that you purchase
a copy of <u>The Angle of Incidence.</u>
This slim volume (paperback, price
$1.50, Warroad Historical Society,
Warroad, Minn. 56763) is a master-
piece in helping the visitor understand the Angle's heritage, and
the love its residents have for
"the surveyor's error." Learn
about the Indian's War Road, the
Falcon, the Magic Garden, and more.
All are part of the history of an
exceptional section of our nation.

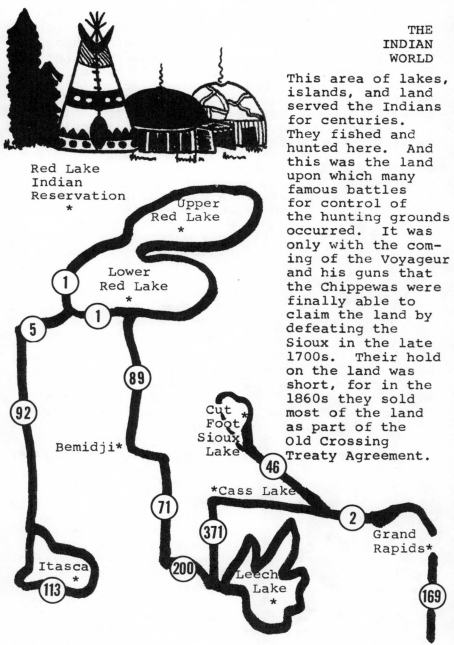

THE
INDIAN
WORLD

This area of lakes, islands, and land served the Indians for centuries. They fished and hunted here. And this was the land upon which many famous battles for control of the hunting grounds occurred. It was only with the coming of the Voyageur and his guns that the Chippewas were finally able to claim the land by defeating the Sioux in the late 1700s. Their hold on the land was short, for in the 1860s they sold most of the land as part of the Old Crossing Treaty Agreement.

Red Lake
Indian
Reservation
*

Upper
Red Lake
*

Lower
Red Lake
*

Cut
Foot
Sioux
Lake
*

Bemidji*

*Cass Lake

Grand
Rapids*

Itasca
*

Leech
Lake
*

To Mille Lacs*

67

No one knows when the first Indian tribe arrived in the Great Lakes area. However, it is known that the Sioux (Dakota) Indians had been living in what is now northcentral Minnesota for hundreds of years before the Chippewa (Ojibway) moved westward from the Atlantic coast into the area. The Dakotas (meaning "friend" or "ally") and the Chippewa could not communicate. They had no common language base, their cultural patterns were quite different, and both wanted control of the rich fishing and hunting grounds in what is now the Superior National Forest area. A continuing war developed between the tribes. For hundreds of years they were evenly matched, and the land sustained both tribes. It was during this period that the name Dakota gradually became Sioux (a name given them by their enemies and meaning "like a snake").

The tribes had different living styles. The Chippewa built dome-shaped houses made of bark, which they called wigwams. Flowing flower patterns enlivened wigwams, canoes, dishes, baskets, and beadwork.

The Sioux lived in earth covered dwellings which later evolved into tepees for the winter months and bark-covered lodges for the summer season. Much of their artwork shows a strong, primitive character with the geometric beadwork outstandingly attractive.

CHIPPEWA

68

French Canadian fur traders arrived in the north woods during the 17th and 18th centuries. With their coming, the evenly matched battle shifted. The Chippewa began to trade fur pelts for guns. The repeating rifle sounded a death knoll for the Sioux as the Chippewa drove them to the plains in the southern section of Minnesota.

The Sioux main food source had been the buffalo (which had roamed the state in herds over 20 miles wide). As fur demands increased, the buffalo began to be hunted and in the mid-1800s became almost extinct. The Sioux turned to farming, an endeavor which they had long regarded as "women's work."

As the white man began to settle Minnesota they soon learned to recognize the Sioux and Chip- pewa. Sioux were noted for their lack of guns, their war paint and war bonnets. The Chippewa wore bear claw necklaces, carried guns and bandelier bags (for carrying shot).

SIOUX

About 90% of the Indians in Minnesota today are Chippewa, most living on reservation land. The Sioux were driven out of the state in 1863. Very few have returned.

NW-Mille Lacs

When you walk into the great hall at the
Mille Lacs-Kathio Indian Museum time is reversed.
You will be standing in the middle of a Chippewa
Indian Village of about 1750. Life size dioramas
illustrate the activities of the Sioux and
Chippewa during the four seasons of their year.
The Museum has some excellent craft exhibits and
does an exceptional job of defining and contrast-
ing the different life styles of Minnesota's
two major Indian tribes--the Chippewa and the
Sioux.

Location: Hwy. 169 on the southwestern
            shore of Lake Mille Lacs
Hours: May 1 through September from
            10 am to 6 pm. Closed on
            Mondays.
Fees: Adults ($1.00), children (25¢),
            no charge for children under 16
            when accompanied by an adult

Restoration work is in progress to uncover
a prehistoric, fortified Indian village. Come
watch the work progress. So far, ricing pits
and burial mounds have been found.

Location: Mille Lacs-Kathio State Park
            on the southwestern shore of
            Lake Mille Lacs
Hours: Daily
Note: Lake Mille Lacs can be dangerous.
            Private small, outboards are not
            recommended. Boaters are advised
            to rent vehicles from boating
            organizations along the lake
            shore.

Indian legends are still told of the violent tribal wars which were fought for control of northwestern Minnesota. Visit the <u>Chippewa National Forest</u> and ask directions to the <u>Turtle and Snake Mound</u>. It serves as a present day reminder of a battle that was fought at least 250 years ago.

For years, the Sioux had controlled the forest. The land was wonderful for hunting and fishing. The Chippewas decided to wage war on the Sioux. For they, too, wanted the land. Chippewas swept into the Sioux camp, they fought fiercely, but were defeated. On the spot where the battle had taken place, the victorious Sioux molded a large turtle (about 25 feet wide and 30 feet long) from the earth. Its head pointed north to show the direction in which the defeated braves had fled. For over a month all was quiet in the forest. The Turtle Mound stood as a memorial to a victorious battle.

In late summer, the Chippewas struck again. This time they were better organized. Still smarting from their last defeat, they outfought the Sioux and massacred the Sioux--to the last man. The last man escaped.

When the Chippewa noticed the turtle mound they, too, knew its significance. They built a snake around the turtle, with its head pointing south (to signify the direction Chippewas would take for future conquests).

As the Chippewa braves were building the snake, the squaws went to a nearby lake for water. There they found the last Sioux, unconscious, with a badly injured foot. The Squaws revived him and helped the man escape. From that day on, the lake has been known as "Cut Foot Sioux Lake!"

This story has been called a campfire legend by some. In any case, the Turtle and Snake Mound is there.

Location: Highway 46 at County Road 35

Bring binoculars and hope for a glance at an American Bald Eagle. It is said that over 1/4 of all the American Bald Eagles remaining in the United States nest in the Chippewa National Forest.

Location: A particularly good spot for viewing the magnificent birds is from the shores of Cass Lake.

Most of us will never have the opportunity to explore the source of either the Nile or the Amazon—the world's two longest rivers. But, the source of the world's third longest river is in Minnesota. Rock hop across the beginning of the mighty Mississippi! It's fun!

Location: A short walk from the parking lot at Itasca State Park
Hours: Daily
Fees: Permit required. See p. 124 .

Itasca State Park is one of Minnesota's loveliest and most attractively maintained facilities. There are foot trails, interpretive walks, a buffalo herd, park naturalists, and marvelous camping/boating/fishing/picnicing facilities.

Location: Hwys. 200 and 71
Hours: Open year-round or as long as the roads remain passable in the wintertime.

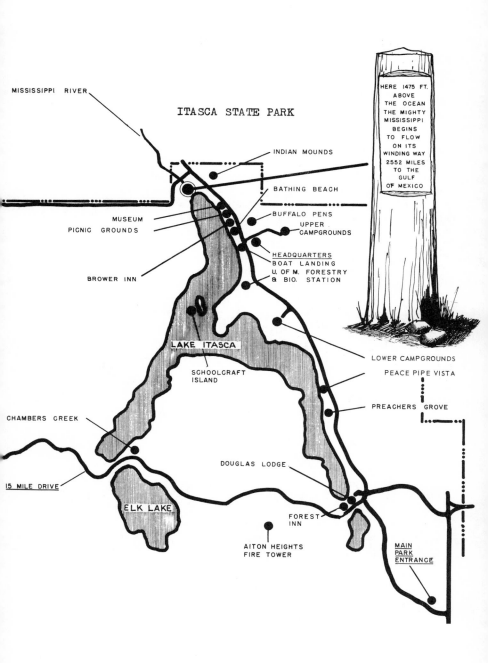

ITASCA STATE PARK

MISSISSIPPI RIVER

INDIAN MOUNDS

BATHING BEACH

MUSEUM

PICNIC GROUNDS

BUFFALO PENS

UPPER CAMPGROUNDS

HEADQUARTERS
BOAT LANDING
U. OF M. FORESTRY
& BIO. STATION

BROWER INN

LOWER CAMPGROUNDS

PEACE PIPE VISTA

LAKE ITASCA

SCHOOLCRAFT ISLAND

PREACHERS GROVE

CHAMBERS CREEK

DOUGLAS LODGE

15 MILE DRIVE

ELK LAKE

FOREST INN

MAIN PARK ENTRANCE

AITON HEIGHTS FIRE TOWER

HERE 1475 FT.
ABOVE
THE OCEAN
THE MIGHTY
MISSISSIPPI
BEGINS
TO FLOW
ON ITS
WINDING WAY
2552 MILES
TO THE
GULF
OF MEXICO

Courtesy Itasca State Park.

73

The <u>Red Lake Indian Reservation</u> is a block
of Indian owned land and water areas. Visitors
are welcome to tour the fish hatchery, saw mill,
and fishing villages. Personal fishing is
by permit only and accompanied by an Indian
Guide. Remember that this is not state owned
land--it is home to more than 1,000 families.

Permits are sold so that families may go
wild ricing within the Red Lake Reservation area.
Ricing boats are poled through the wild rice bed.
Two tapered flails are used; one to bend the
rice stems over the boat, the other to tap the
ripened rice into the wide-bottomed canoe.
When you return home with the rice, it should be
parched over an open fire (or in a slow oven) to
loosen the hulls. The grain is then poured into a
wide pit (or plastic lined sand box?) where someone stomps off the outer hulls. Then winnow the
grain, separating the rice from the loosened
hulls, and bag the delicious, gourmet wild rice.
An excellent color reproduction of the Chippewa
Indians completing the wild ricing process is
available through the Minnesota Department of
Conservation, 350 Centennial Building, St. Paul,
Minnesota 55101. "Wild Rice Harvest" was
painted by Patrick Des Jarlait who grew up on
the Red Lake Reservation. It is exceptional.

Distance between <u>Brainerd</u>
and <u>Detroit Lakes</u> is
approximately 90 miles;
between <u>Detroit Lakes</u> and
<u>Bemidji</u> is approximately
90 miles; between <u>Brainerd</u>
and <u>Bemidji</u> is approximately
100 miles.

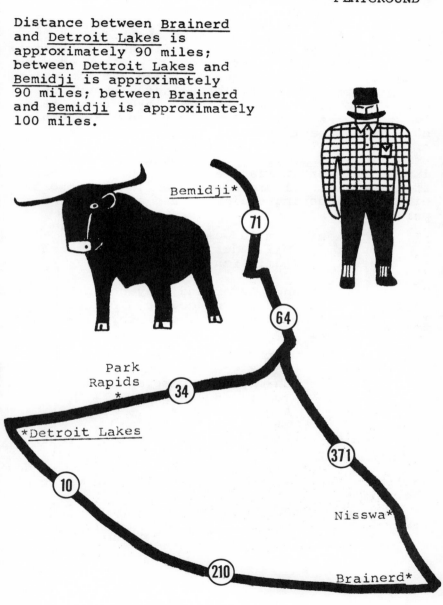

Bemidji*

71

64

Park
Rapids
*

34

*Detroit Lakes

371

10

Nisswa*

210

Brainerd*

The legend of Paul Bunyan and Babe, his
Blue Ox, is said to have leaped directly from
the pen of an imaginative writer into the hearts
of northcentral Americans.

Midwesterners say that Paul and Babe
created the thousands of lakes in this area by
stomping across Minnesota. Their huge footprints
later filled with water. Today, whether they be
considered the footprints of a man and his ox or
the product of a benevolent glacial sheet put
down during the Ice Age, these lakes serve as a
modern-day Paul Bunyan's playground. Everything
here is just a little bit larger than life.

The Paul Bunyan Center features the giant
lumberjack--or at least a 23 foot high carved
statue of him. There is also an interesting exhibit of lumbering equipment and an amusement
park nearby.

> Location: 1 mile west of Brainerd
> Hours: Daily during the summer months
> Fees: Admission charged

Zoom! Around and around they go on America's
fastest 3 mile road racing course. Donnybrooke
International Speedway provides a thrill a minute
for fans of all ages.

> Location: North of Brainerd on Hwy. 371
> Hours: Check your newspaper, the Brainerd
>   Chamber of Commerce, or Donnybrooke
>   for racing dates.
> Fees: Admission charged

Feeding the tame deer is the big attraction
at Deer Forest. There are bear, otter, ducks,
geese and other wild animals in a natural, wooded
setting. This is an excellent place to visit with
the animals at close range.

> Location: Watch for signs near Nisswa
> Hours: Daily during the summer months
> Fees: Admission charged

   Lumbertown, U.S.A. is a replica of an 1870
lumbering town. Besides exploring the trading
post, children will enjoy going down to the levee
at the Blueberry River to see (and perhaps ride?)
the riverboat. There is a replica of the first
Northern Pacific railroad train which provides
rides around Lumbertown.

Location: 12 miles northwest of Brainerd
             at Pine Beach on Gull Lake.
             Follow Hwy. 371 signs for 4 miles
             to Lumbertown turnoff. Proceed
             for 8 miles to the site.
Hours: Daily from mid-June to Labor Day,
             10 am to 7 pm
Fees: Adults (50¢), children (25¢)

Climb aboard the exciting <u>Fargo Stagecoach</u> and travel back to the old days when mail and passengers careened over the countryside. When children tire of this activity, the area also offers picnic groves, row-boating, and the ever popular paddle boats.

Location: Fort Detroit, Detroit Lakes
Hours: Daily during the summer months
Fees: Admission charged

The <u>Becker County Museum</u> displays one of the first log cabins built in the area. There is also an interesting gun collection (including a first model Smith and Wesson), a natural history exhibit, and a small, but superb, collection of Indian beadwork.

Location: County Courthouse, Detroit Lakes
Hours: Monday to Friday from 2 to 5 pm
Fees: Free

The legend of Paul Bunyan lives on in
Bemidji. Children enjoy the huge statues of
Paul and Babe, his Blue Ox. A nearby Information Center contains Paul's toothbrush, shoe-
horn, and other "useful" items from the world
of the northland's mightiest lumberjack. There
is a lake and amusement park nearby.

    Location: Lakefront, Bemidji
    Hours: Daily during the summer months
    Fees: Free

THE TWIN CITIES
MINNEAPOLIS AND ST. PAUL

Minnesota has two modern, metropolitan centers within 10 miles of each other. We are so impressed with the resources of these two cities that we have written a book about what to see and do within them. We recommend An Uncommon Guide to the Twin Cities (paperback, $2.95, Tailored Tours Publications, Box 24222, Minneapolis, Minn. 55424) to help you explore both Minneapolis and St. Paul.

However, if you have only a day to spend in each city, we provide the following ideas for what we consider to be among the not-to-be-missed attractions of this marvelous area.

A DAY IN MINNEAPOLIS

Begin with a drive around the city's lovely lakes (Lake Harriet, Lake Calhoun, and Lake of the Isles). Then spend an hour at the Minneapolis Institute of Art. Housed within the Institute is the Children's Theatre. This is probably the best children's theatre in the country--go to a production, even without a child, and enjoy yourself. (Museum is at 201 E. 24 St.) Next take a trip to the top of the Foshay Tower to view the city (821 Marquette Ave.), and a visit to the new Walker Art Center (Hennepin at Lyndale). Take time for lunch and a stroll along Nicollet Mall, the city's main shopping area. Late afternoon will find you exploring the University of Minnesota's Natural History Museum (University & 17th Ave., SE) before dinner and an evening at the Guthrie Theatre (725 Vineland Place), the Minnesota Orchestra (Northrop Auditorium, U of M), or a feature sports attraction at the Metropolitan Stadium (Rt. 494 and 24th St., S.).

A DAY IN ST. PAUL

Begin the day with a tour of Minnesota's beautiful <u>State Capitol</u> (University Avenue) and then walk down the hill to the <u>St. Paul Arts and Science Museum</u>'s fascinating collections. The <u>Indian God of Peace</u> serves as a reminder of the Indian's heritage in Minnesota (Court House, 4th and Wabasha). Lunch in St. Paul and spend a few minutes shop-browsing along <u>West 5th Street.</u> Begin the afternoon with a tour of the <u>Ramsey House</u> (265 S. Exchange St.) and then drive along St. Paul's loveliest street--<u>Summit Avenue</u> (the Governor's Residence is located at 1006 Summit. It is not open to the public). Spend late after- noon at the <u>Como Park Zoo and Conservatory</u> (Hamline and Midway Parkway). After dinner we recommend a presentation by the <u>St. Paul Opera Association,</u> the <u>St. Paul Chamber Orchestra</u> (Crawford Livings- ton Theatre), the <u>Minnesota Orchestra</u> (College of St. Catherine), or a sports event at the <u>Metropolitan Stadium</u> (8001 Cedar Avenue).

HALF A DAY BETWEEN THE TWIN CITIES

Take a picnic lunch to <u>Fort Snelling</u> and tour one of the first military outposts west of the Mississippi (Hwy. 55, south of the Twin Cities). Continue across the bridge to the restored <u>Sibley</u> (built 1835) and <u>Faribault</u> (built 1836) <u>Houses</u> (Mendota, Route 13).

SOUTHEASTERN MINNESOTA

Over 100 miles of breathtakingly beautiful scenery stretch along the Mississippi River's banks. High bluffs, a steamboat, riverfront towns, and geological wonders await modern-day adventurers.

Although the area's history was directly related to trade and travel along the Mississippi, groups of settlers began to discover inland fields in the 1850s. One of these small towns, Rochester, was to emerge as one of America's outstanding medical centers.

Southeastern Minnesota is a fascinating area to visit. We hope you enjoy exploring as much as we enjoyed researching the following tours.

82

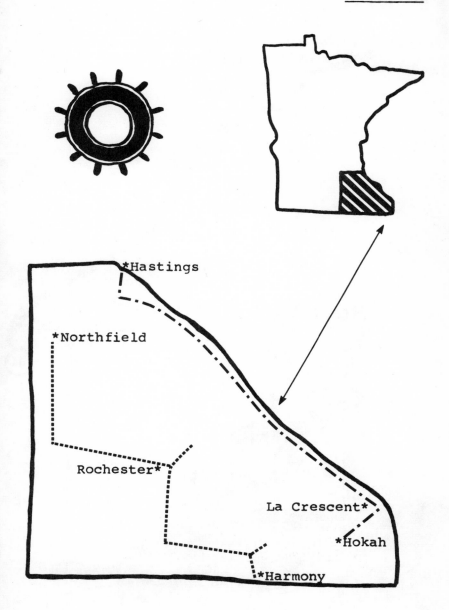

SOUTHEASTERN
MINNESOTA

*Hastings

*Northfield

Rochester*

La Crescent*

*Hokah

*Harmony

83

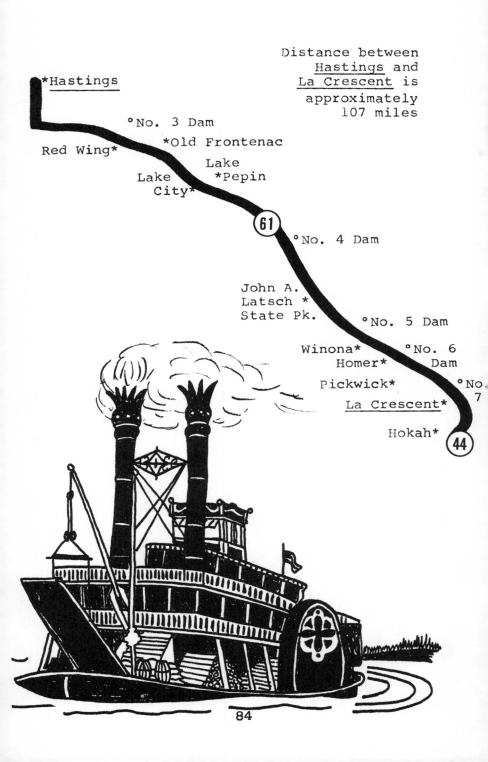

Distance between
<u>Hastings</u> and
<u>La Crescent</u> is
approximately
107 miles

*Hastings

°No. 3 Dam

Red Wing*   *Old Frontenac

                   Lake
Lake   *Pepin
City*

(61)

°No. 4 Dam

John A.
Latsch *
State Pk.

°No. 5 Dam

Winona*   °No. 6
  Homer*   Dam

Pickwick*   °No.
                              7
<u>La Crescent</u>*

        Hokah*   (44)

As the mighty riverboats travelled up and down the Mississippi, many towns began to grow upon the shores. During the 1800s, river trade from New Orleans up the Mississippi to the Twin Cities began to increase. The products and needs of an expanding state made the waterfront towns centers for meeting, trading, and transit.

The Le Duc Mansion is a memorial to American Victorian Gothic architecture. It was built in 1856 by a Civil War General who returned to Hastings several times during the war to supervise the mansion's construction.

Location: 17th and Vermillion Streets
Hours: Summer months only, by
            appointment
Fees: Admission charged

Hastings is a town racing to remember its past. A number of groups are trying to save some of the town's early buildings--we wish them success! One enterprising gentleman bought an old house which was going to be torn down to make way for a school expansion.
The big frame mansion was moved several blocks and now resides in quiet elegance on its new site. As you drive by, recall that this house was built in 1899.

Location: 1007 Sibley Street, Hastings
Note: THIS IS A PRIVATE DWELLING.   IT
            IS NOT OPEN TO THE PUBLIC.

The Ramsey Mill site serves as a reminder of the city's early flour milling days.

Location: Vermillion River and Rt. 75
Hours: Daily
Fees: Free
Note: The Mill is gone, however the
            site provides an interesting spot
            for a walk.

85

Chimney Rock is said to be 15,000 years old.
That is an old, old rock! This geological oddity
served as a marker for Indians and early settlers.
You might enjoy finding it atop a hill where this
sandstone and limestone structure stands as a
sentinel from a prehistoric era.

Location: Hwy. 61, 6 miles south of
Hastings to 220th Street. Turn
right on 220th Street for 3 miles.
Turn right onto Joan Road for
1/2 mile and there's the rock.

Just north of Red Wing, almost hidden by a
high fence, is Tower View. Professor Alexander
Anderson built the house and Tower Laboratory in
1917. Following his graduation from Minnesota
State College, Dr. Anderson studied and taught
in Germany and at Columbia University. He discovered the methods for expanding cereal grains
which led to the commercial products, Puffed Wheat
and Puffed Rice. After half a lifetime of teaching,
researching, and a profitable coordination with
Quaker Oats, Professor Anderson decided to return
to the boyhood farm where he had grown up. Tower
View was built where a farmhouse once stood.

Location: A few miles north of Red Wing on
Hwy. 61. Watch for the Tower.
Note: THIS IS A PRIVATE RESIDENCE. IT
IS NOT OPEN TO THE PUBLIC.

The Red Wing Pottery Company is dead, but the
Red Wing Pottery Showroom still sells remainders
of that lovely hand painted pottery.

Location: Just off Hwy. 61, Red Wing
Hours: Daily from 9 am to 5 pm

Red Wing Pottery dominated the town's economic
destiny for many years. Then, on June 1, 1967 the
workers walked out of the factory in a strike for
higher wages. Management was unable to meet the
strikers demands and the plant closed. It was an
economic blow to all concerned. Everyone lost.
The town is only now, almost 4 years after the
strike began, beginning to wage a strenuous economic
comeback.

The <u>Mississippi River Dams and Locks</u> are fun to travel and almost as much fun to watch. During the course of the route between Hastings and La Crescent, the elevation ranges between 675 feet and 639 feet. Watch the boats travel "up and down hill" on the river.

Locations:	#3 Dam, Hastings, elev. 675'
	#4 Dam, Kellogg, elev. 667'
	#5 Dam, opposite John A. Latsch State Park, elev. 660'
	#5A Dam, Minnesota City, elev. 651'
	#6 Dam, Lamoille, elev. 645'
	#7 Dam, near LaCrescent, elev.639'
Hours:	Daily during the summer months
Fees:	Free to watch

<u>Old Frontenac</u> residents build and buy the best bird houses! Our favorite, to date, is an immense, red-roofed gabled mansion. Try to find it, you'll be amazed by the careful workmanship.

The entire Minnesota/Wisconsin Mississippi River Border area is a bird watcher's delight. The "Mississippi Flyway" serves as the Interstate Highway for migrating birds.

A boat ride on <u>Lake Pepin</u> is a delightful way to punctuate a drive down river.

Location:	Lake City Harbor Entrance
Hours:	Daily during summer months, rides at 2 and 7 pm
Fees:	Adults ($2.00), teenagers ($1.25), children (75¢)

Serious rock hounds enjoy beach walks near Lake City. Tabulate coral, algae jasper, agates, and "pretty rocks" cover the beaches. Children tend to finish the walk with pockets laden with treasures.

Location:	Beaches and gravel pits in and near Lake City
Hours:	Daily
Fees:	Free

Commercial strawberry growers offer several acres of berries for local sale. Ask in a service station or drug store for the address of a nearby strawberry nursery and buy a few quarts of fresh-picked berries.

Location: Nurseries in and near Lake City
Hours: Early summer months
Note: Try to save some berries to savour at the

John A. Latsch State Park. This is a particularly good place for River watching. The best viewing spots are high atop the 3 limestone bluffs. Indians, rivermen, and lumbermen knew these bluffs and used them as route markers. Today's traveller looks down upon a fascinating and ever changing collage of 20th century life upon "ole Miss".

Location: Hwy. 61
Hours: Daily during summer months
Fees: Permit required. See p. 124.

Winona (an Indian name for "first born daughter") was founded to serve the riverboats. Its business streets and many of the churches and homes are reminiscent of the 19th century. This is a town of tall church spires, colleges, and imposing granite bluffs. In the mid-1850s, the town was crowded with loggers, millhands, and rivermen all working to meet the growing demands for lumber. The present city rests upon thousands of tons of sawdust which had been used to reinforce the sandy soil. As lumbering declined, grain milling began and Winona remained a significant riverboat port. When steamboating on the Mississippi ended, the resourceful Winonans turned to their own granite and limestone bluffs and provided a new economic future for their town.

The Julius C. Wilkie is Minnesota's only wood hulled steamboat. Built in 1898, rebuilt in 1938, and docked in 1956, this vessel has become a Museum which commemorates the Golden Age of Steamboating. The whole family will enjoy the engines, wheels, bells, sights and sounds that surge through this dock-side, shipboard museum.

> Location: Levee Park, Front Street, Winona
> Hours: May 1 to October 1, Monday through Saturday from 9 am to 5 pm, Sundays and holidays from 10 am to 6 pm.
> Fees: Admission charged.

Levee Park was once a busy steamboat landing. It is now a quiet park and provides the visitor with an opportunity to turn from the bustling city and view the quiet movements of America's mightiest river.

> Location: Front Street, Winona
> Hours: Daily
> Fees: Free

There are logging and lumbering exhibits at the Winona County Historical Society Museum.

Location: 125 West 5 St., Winona
Hours: Closed in August. Otherwise, open
              from Monday-Friday, 9 am to 5 pm
Fees: Free

The Bunnell House, built in 1850, was the first permanent settler's home in the area.

Location: Just off Rt. 61, Homer
Hours: Summer months only, Monday through
              Saturday from 1-5 pm, Sunday from
              2-6 pm
Fees: Admission charged

A visit to Emil Lier's Otter Sanctuary is such fun! Mr. Lier is a noted otter authority who presents unusual trained otter exhibitions.

Location: Off Rt. 61, south of Homer
Hours: Summer months only.
Fees: Admission charged

Look for faces in the towering bluffs as you drive south on Rt. 61. Our favorite is Queen's Bluff. Watch for her face, all rimmed in leafy splendor.

La Crescent spells and smells S-P-R-I-N-G! John Samuel Harris, Minnesota's own Johnny Appleseed, planted acres of seeds in 1857 and the apple valley came to life. A few years later, seed from Russia and other northern climates was added. La Crescent became the apple growing center of the upper midwest. Drive through the area in the Spring to see the blossoms and smell their fragrance. We also visit during harvest time to stock up on just picked, juicy fruit.

Location: Rt. 61. Orchards are in the
              hills surrounding the town.
Hours: Daily
Fees: Free

If time permits, drive through the rolling countryside between Hokah and Caledonia. It is beautiful.

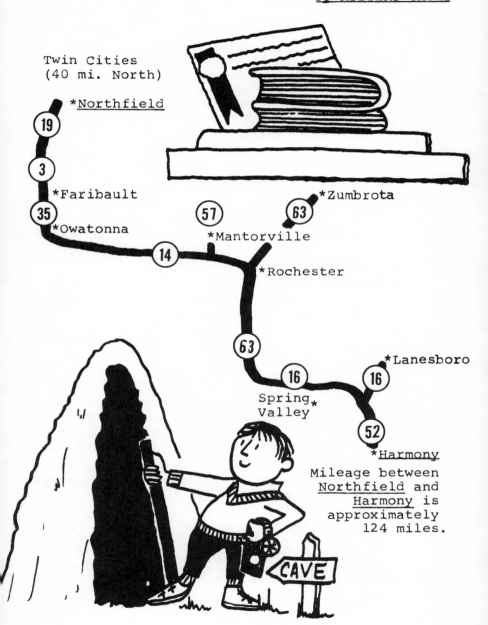

FROM COLLEGE TOWN TO MYSTERY CAVES

Twin Cities
(40 mi. North)

*Northfield

(19)

(3)

*Faribault

(35)

*Owatonna

(57)

*Mantorville

(63)

*Zumbrota

(14)

*Rochester

(63)

(16)

(16)

*Lanesboro

Spring
Valley *

(52)

*Harmony

Mileage between
Northfield and
Harmony is
approximately
124 miles.

CAVE

Northfield is an exceptional city! It is one of the few communities in the nation which has <u>two</u> outstanding liberal arts colleges. In addition, the bravery of its citizens marked the end of a terror-filled era for all midwesterners.

Norwegian Lutheran pioneers came to southeastern Minnesota and started a community and a school years before Minnesota became a state. Northfield was their home; <u>St. Olaf College</u> is an outgrowth of their school. The college was formed to keep the "young people in contact with the church, while giving them a liberal arts education."

Drive through the St. Olaf Campus and note the interesting contrast between the gray limestone castle-like structure dominating the hill and the striking, glass-faced dormitories. Try to visit the <u>College Center</u>. (An art exhibit usually lines the walls.) Children and adults alike are captivated by the <u>Werenskiold Doors</u> and great, contemporary Scandinavian fireplace.

Our favorite reason for a trip to St. Olaf is to hear their choir and band. Call or write to learn the concert dates and plan your visit.

Location: St. Olaf Ave., about a mile west of Northfield Center
Hours: Daily
Fees: Free to visit

<u>Carleton College</u> dominates the east side of Northfield. This outstanding school has a long history of excellence. We recommend a leisurely walk through the campus to fully appreciate its interesting architecture and setting.

Location: Off Rt. 19 on Northfield's northeast hill
Hours: Daily
Fees: Free to visit

The <u>Carleton College Arboretum</u> is lovely. If you have a quiet, sunlit, afternoon, you might enjoy this 6 mile, self-guided nature trail.

Location: Carleton College, off Rt. 19

September 7, 1876 is a red letter day in
Northfield's history. For, on that date, the
<u>Jesse James Gang</u> rode into town to rob the bank!
They couldn't open the safe. A few minutes later,
4 people were dead and the gang had fled. The
manhunt was on. At its height, 1,000 men had been
deputized and were searching for the gang. Within
14 days, the entire gang had been caught--except
for Jesse and his brother, Frank. There is much
speculation that the 2 brothers remained hidden
in one of the caves near the border.

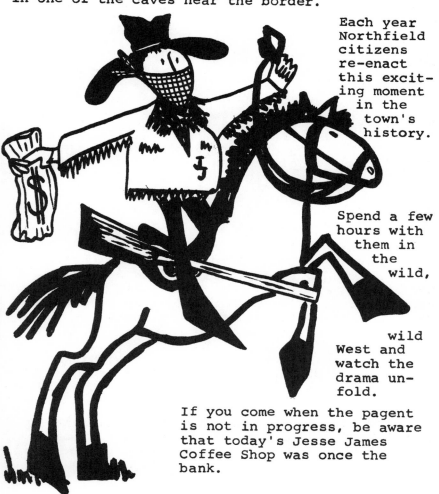

Each year
Northfield
citizens
re-enact
this excit-
ing moment
in the
town's
history.

Spend a few
hours with
them in
the
wild,

wild
West and
watch the
drama un-
fold.

If you come when the pagent
is not in progress, be aware
that today's Jesse James
Coffee Shop was once the
bank.

Faribault began as a fur trading post. Some reminders of its early days can be seen at the <u>Alexander Faribault Museum</u>. It was the first frame house in town and, according to the records, was built for $4,000 with lumber carted all the way from St. Paul.

Location: 12 N.E. 1st Ave., Faribault
Hours: May 1 to October 1 from 1-5 pm
Fees: Admission charged

The town grew both because of its location and its fertile soil. Pack a picnic and plan to be amazed by Faribault's two outstanding flower spectaculars. The <u>Brand Peony Farm</u>'s display shows over 20,000 blooms at one time. Dates: late May to mid-June. <u>Lehman Gardens</u> is one of the country's leading chrysanthemum growers. Their show is yearly from September 15 to November 1. Both are free and are known by avid gardeners throughout the country.

The <u>Shattuck Military School</u> and <u>St. Mary's Preparatory School</u>, two exceptional secondary educational institutions, are also located here.

Tours are conducted through the <u>Faribault Woolen Mill</u>. There is also a "seconds" store where you may find a bargain.

Location: 1500 N.W. 2nd Ave., N.
Hours: Tours conducted Monday through
             Friday at 10 am and 2 pm
Fees: Free
Note: Children under 12 must be ac-
             companied by a parent.

<u>Treasure Cave</u> is any blue cheese lover's idea of a good time. The cheese is aged within a series of caves, through which tours are conducted. Blue cheese and crackers are served at the end of the tour.

Location: 222 3rd St., N.E., Faribault
Hours: Monday-Friday at 9:30, 11:30, 1, 3
Fees: Free
Note: The caves are cool. Bring a
             sweater or jacket.

Come during banking hours and look, really look, at the <u>Security Bank of Owatonna</u>. In 1907 a group of businessmen hired one of America's outstanding architects to design a bank. Louis Sullivan did a superb job. Now, over half a century later, the building still ranks at or near the top of any list of Minnesota's outstanding structures.

Location: North Cedar Street, Owatonna
Hours: Monday-Friday from 9 am to 2 pm
Fees: Free

<u>Mantorville</u> is one of Minnesota's oldest towns. It began as a way-station for the Dakota Stagecoach. Today's residents are eager to bring back the gas light era. We look forward to Mantorville's return to yesteryear. In the meantime, it is interesting to watch their restoration progress.

Location: Hwy. 57 a short distance north of
            Hwy. 14.

Bring the family and walk through <u>Minnesota's only covered bridge.</u> This latticed, wooden-truss type bridge was used for over 50 years. In 1932 it was replaced by a "modern" bridge and the wooden structure was moved to the Goodhue County Fairgrounds. In its second life, the bridge served as a poultry exhibit building and then as a refreshment stand. After a good deal of work, a committee made the necessary arrangements to return the bridge to the river. In 1970, a crew (which was larger than the number of men necessary to build the bridge!) moved the fir and oak structure back to the banks of the Zumbro River and the bridge began its third life. It looks as though it had never left the riverside.

Location: Zumbrota
Hours: Daily
Fees: Free

In the 1880s, Rochester, Minnesota was little
more than a crossroad village surrounded by the
prairie. To this collection of houses, came a
doctor, a nun and a tornado.

The "little doctor" (as he was to become
affectionately known) treated scores of people
injured by the high wind; the nun pledged her
Sisters of St. Francis to nurse the injured back
to health. A short time later, the concept for
what was to become the world famous Mayo Clinic
was born.

Rochester's dedication to the Mayo Clinic
was overwhelming from the beginning. Dr. William
Worrell Mayo and his two sons began to treat all
who needed medical attention--regardless of their
ability to pay. Not only did these men understand
the need for superb clinical medicine, but they
had the skill to learn and teach new concepts
(often adding their own significant improvements
to the new concept).

During the 1890s, the railroad began to
stop in Rochester. Patients who had heard of the
Mayos arrived by train from around the world. By
the 1920s, over 20,000 patients were being treated
each year. In 1970, the Clinic served more than
200,000 patients!

A marvelous biography of the Mayo men and
their part in modern medicine has been written.
We highly recommend The Doctors Mayo by Helen
Clapesattle (paperback, $.95, Pocket Books).

The Mayo Clinic dominates present-day
Rochester. If there were time to see only one
place while in town, we would go directly to the
Mayo Clinic Tour. All participants first see a
25 minute movie which outlines the Clinic's

history, philosophy and present-day functions.
This provides useful background information as
you begin an escorted tour of the facilities.

    Location: Tours begin from Judd Hall
                located adjacent to the elevators
                in the subway (underground walk-
                way) of the Mayo Building
    Hours: Tours are conducted Monday through
                Friday at 10 am and 2 pm
    Fees: Free

    All the art work in the Clinic reflects an
aspect of man's activities, achievements, and
philosophies. The impressive collection of
sculpture, murals, and other art forms is
pleasingly displayed throughout the Clinic Complex.

    Dedicated in 1928 to the American Soldier, the
Rochester Carillon continues to delight all within
listening range. There are 23 bells which weigh
more than 18 tons pealing forth Gregorian chimes
and hymns.

    Location: The Plummer Building
    Hours: Bells rung on Mondays at 7 pm,
                Wednesdays and Fridays at noon
    Fees: Free
    Note: To best enjoy the music, we sug-
                gest that you be about 200-500
                feet from the Plummer Building.
                Try to listen in an open area.

    One of our favorite quiet spots in Rochester
is the Mayo Memorial. Within a natural setting,
a semicircular amphitheatre of land serves as the
memorial area. The bronze statues of Drs. "Will"
and "Charlie" are magnificent examples of portrait
sculpture. In a city dedicated to life, take a
moment to know these great men.

    Location: Memorial Park
    Hours: Daily
    Fees: Free

Learn about open-heart surgery and see how medicine was practiced at the turn of the century --all at the Mayo Medical Museum.

Location: Adjacent to the Parking Ramp
            exit in the Damon Building
Hours: Monday through Friday from 9 am
            to 9 pm, Saturday from 9 am to
            5 pm, Sunday from 1 pm to 5 pm.
Fees: Free

A fully furnished log cabin is only one of the reasons to tour the fascinating Olmsted County Historical Society Museum.

Location: 214 3rd Ave., S.W.
Hours: Monday through Friday from 9 am to
            5 pm, Saturday from noon to 4 pm
Fees: Free

Mayowood was the home of Drs. Charles W. and Charles H. Mayo. Their 38 room mansion looks much as it did when the families lived here. There are lovely antiques, a Napoleon Room, and articles relating to the Mayo men. The peace and tranquility surrounding the home and grounds will remain with you long after the tour ends.

Location: All tours depart by bus from the Olmsted County Historical Society Building, 214 3rd Ave., S.W.
Hours: May through October, tours given Wednesday through Saturday at 1 and 3 pm, Sunday at noon, 2 and 4 pm.
Fees: Adults ($1.75), children ($1.00)
Note: Please write for reservations in advance.

St. Mary's Hospital offers tours through the facilities. Founded by the Sisters of St. Francis, St. Mary's has grown with the Mayo Clinic.

Hours: Tours given Monday-Friday at 3 pm
Fees: Free

The Rochester Art Center has a full program of exhibits, concerts, and classes. The building, near Mayo Park, is fun for browsing.

Location: 320 East Center Street
Hours: 10-5, Tuesday through Saturday, 1-5, Sunday
Fees: Free
Note: Plan to attend one of the Sunday evening concerts.

The Rochester Civic Theatre and the Rochester Symphony Orchestra provide varied and interesting entertainment. If you will be in Rochester for more than a day, we recommend you phone their box offices and try to schedule an evening of theatre or music while in town.

Canada Geese are alive and thriving in the heated splendor of Silver Lake. No matter what the season, these big birds (14-18 pounds) are admired, fed, cared for, and talked about by the area's townspeople and visitors. Bring a bag of stale bread and join the fun.

Location: 13th Street and North Broadway, Rochester
Hours: Daily
Fees: Free

The Hemp Antique Vehicles Museum traces the development of automobiles from a 1903 Ford on-ward. There is also an interesting assortment of antique farm machinery and the Dr. C. W. Mayo collection of horse drawn carriages.

Location: 1/2 mile south of Rochester on Hwy. 14 at junction of Co. Rds. 34 and 3
Hours: Daily from March-November
Fees: Admission charged

One of Minnesota's oldest stone churches is an interesting destination for a Sunday drive. St. Bridget's Church was built in 1859.

Location: Rt. 63 south of Rochester to Olmsted Co. Rd. 16. Turn left to the church.

The Lanesboro Fish Hatchery is very attractive. Start at the office for a briefing and then take a self-guided walk through the area. You will ab-sorb a great deal of information about the business of raising fish for Minnesota's lakes and streams.

Location: Lanesboro
Hours: Daily during summer months
Fees: Free
Note: This is Minnesota's largest fish hatchery.

Spelunking is a good hobby for southeastern Minnesotans! There are many caves in the area!

Mystery Caves were discovered in 1937. These limestone areas comprise about 1,000 feet of underground passageway. There is the "Garden of the Gods", "Turquoise Lake", and many other "rooms" to see while far underground. Be aware of the fossil-rich limestone beds separated by gray shale.

Location: Spring Valley, then 6 miles south-east. Watch for signs.
Hours: Daily during summer months
Fees: Admission charged
Note: There are two tours here. We recommend that you wear a sweater or jacket, it's cool in the caves.

Niagara Cave was found in 1924 when three boys were searching for some lost pigs. The pigs were found in the entrance to the cave, taken back to the farmyard, and the boys began to explore "their" find. The areas they found have been re-named. Visit Niagara caves for its stalactites, stalagmites, and fossils as well as "Paul Bunyan's Bed," "the Crystal Wedding Chapel" and other fancifully named passageways. It may help to remember that stalagtites go down, when stalagmites go up!

Location: Off Rt. 139, 5 miles southwest of Harmony
Hours: Year round from 10 am to 4 pm
Fees: Admission charged
Note: Wear a sweater or jacket, it's cool in the cave.

Caves throughout Minnesota are known to have served as hiding places for some of the Wild West Gangs that roamed the prairie. With a well camoflagued entrance, an outlaw gang (and their horses) could effectively hide inside a large cave and elude the posse.

SOUTHWESTERN
MINNESOTA

The Jolly Green Giant lives in southwestern Minnesota! It is indeed appropriate that he would have chosen this corner of Minnesota, with its symmetrical corn fields, its wheat and turkey and dairy farms. This is a bountiful part of the state.

The land was owned by the King of France, who traded it to the King of Spain, who sold it to the United States as part of the Louisiana Purchase. During this time, and for unknown periods before, it had been the property of the plains Indian. As the white man moved west, treaties were formulated with the Dakota Indians (or Sioux as they were to become commonly known). A struggle for equality was waged, the Sioux lost and were driven from Minnesota in 1863. As the Indian danger passed, settlers arrived to farm the prairie, to carve towns and schools from the land, and the brushfire of modern civilization moved westward.

With the founding and settling of towns, came groups and individuals with many backgrounds. Many of these heritages exist today and will be noted as you explore southwestern Minnesota on the following tours:

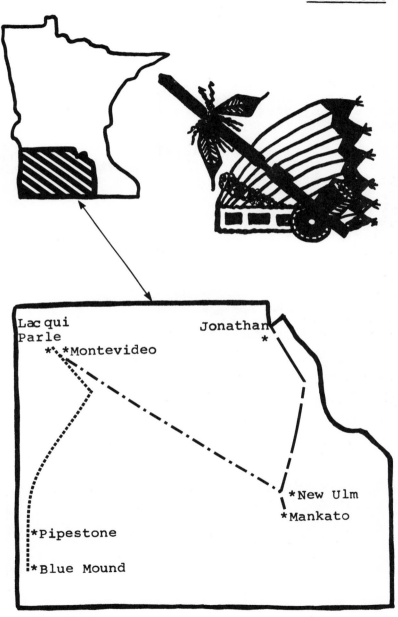

Lac qui
Parle
  *∙.*Montevideo   Jonathan
                                        *

*Pipestone

:*Blue Mound

                                    *New Ulm
                                    *Mankato

105

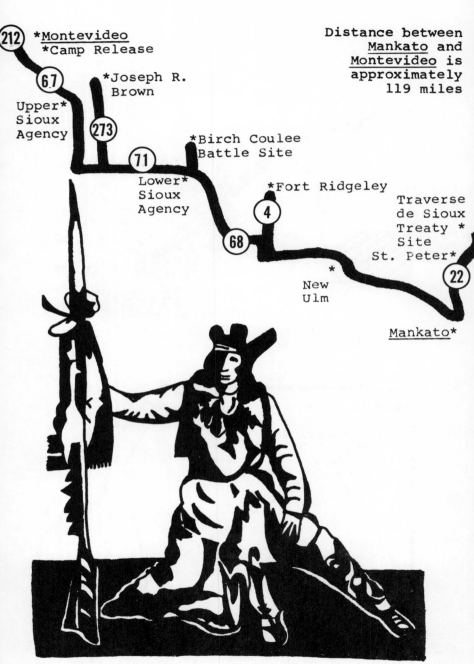

(212) *Montevideo
*Camp Release

Distance between Mankato and Montevideo is approximately 119 miles

(67)

*Joseph R. Brown

Upper* Sioux Agency

(273)

*Birch Coulee Battle Site

(71)

Lower* Sioux Agency

*Fort Ridgeley

(4)

Traverse de Sioux Treaty * Site St. Peter*

(68)

*
New Ulm

(22)

Mankato*

"Dakota chiefs do not fear to die,
They will do what is best for their people."
Chief Little Crow

106

There were 35 Indian Chiefs in full formal
attire and as many United States Military
Officers in full dress. Peace pipes, official
documents, and much good cheer accompanied the
historic days when hundreds of negotiators
descended upon Traverse de Sioux. In a very real
sense, the Great Sioux Uprising began on July 23,
1851 when the Sioux sold nearly 24 million acres
of land in southern Minnesota (and parts of Iowa
and South Dakota) to the United States Government.
The land was sold for 4-1/2¢ an acre. The
United States was to pay for the land over a 20
year period--in gold--payable on or about July 1
of each year.

The Indians maintained a narrow strip of land
to serve as their reservation. All soon realized
it was too little land to sustain tribal life.

After the treaty was ratified, the land was
opened for homesteading. Settlers poured into
the area.

For over 11 years, Indians and pioneers lived
together in relative harmony. The Indians spent
most of their time on the reservation, the
pioneers spent most of their time on or near
their homesteads. Most of the friction which did
occur seems to have been related to the Indians'
feelings that the treaty had been made with "the
white man" rather than with "the government."
When a payment was late, the Sioux assumed that
"the white man (or settler)" should be responsible.

A gold payment was due on July 1, 1862. All
through that hot, dry month the Sioux waited for
their money. Crops had been bad, homesteading
and pelting had driven away most of the game, and
Indian families began to starve. Chiefs came to
the Lower Sioux Agency daily inquiring about the
$71,000. When it was more than 30 days overdue,

107

the Sioux chiefs asked for credit at "the white man's store." Although large shipments of food had recently arrived at the store (in anticipation of the Indian's money), the storekeeper said he would advance no credit. As the Sioux chiefs and their braves turned to leave, they overheard the storekeeper say, "If they are hungry, let them eat grass."

Meanwhile, the American Congress was reluctant to part with the gold because of the extreme financial pressures of the Civil War. After much deliberation, the gold left Washington on August 2, 1862. It would arrive in Minnesota 48 hours after the Sioux Uprising had begun.

Violence erupted on the afternoon of August 17, 1862, when 4 hunger crazed young braves found a nest of eggs on a homesteader's property. Goaded on by one of the braves, another swore he would kill the settler whose property he was not allowed to touch. The eggs were thrown against a rock. As the yolk stained the rock yellow, the braves headed for the settler's cabin. A short time later, 5 settlers were dead and the braves began to realize the implications of their bloody deeds.

All through the night the Indian chiefs met at the home of their hereditary tribal leader, Little Crow. The young men wanted to fight for their ancestral hunting grounds. They argued that the white man had broken his promise. That, coupled with the number of settlers who were away from their farms fighting in the Civil War convinced the younger braves that they had a chance to win the battle. Little Crow was against the move, but popular opinion carried and battle plans began to be made.

The first attack occurred at the <u>Lower Sioux Agency Storehouse</u>. It is said that the first man killed was the storekeeper. When he was found his mouth had been stuffed with grass. Fighting spread across the parched prairieland like a brushfire. <u>New Ulm</u> was attacked on August 19, then again on August 20 and 23. On the 24th, New Ulm's survivors were moved to <u>Mankato</u>.

The fighting continued. After their victory at New Ulm, the Sioux moved on Fort Ridgeley. Many women and children were taken captive and transported to the reservation lands near the present town of Montevideo.

When the fighting broke out in New Ulm, Private Sturgis made the trip from New Ulm to St. Paul, on horseback, in record time. He alerted Governor Ramsey of the catastrophe on Minnesota's prairie. Ramsey acted quickly and appointed Henry Sibley to lead U.S. Troops into the battle area. Sibley headed for St. Peter.

Military strength and weaponry were too much for the Sioux. Sibley and his troops reached Camp Release on September 25, 1862, released the women and children, and took over 300 Indians captive. The war was over.

Although some figures are higher, the most accurate estimate of deaths resulting from the six week prairie war was about 500 persons. As soon as the Indians were taken captive, court martial proceedings began. They moved at a fast pace and, soon, more than 300 Indians had been sentenced to death.

One of the real heroes of the Indian Uprising was Henry Whipple, Episcopal clergyman and the first Bishop of Minnesota. Bishop Whipple had been concerned about injustices to the Indians. Years before the uprising, he had written to President Buchanan about irregularities in the way treaty agreements were being carried out in the territory. He had also written to President Lincoln about similar matters. As Bishop Whipple listened to the court martial proceedings, he decided to ride to Washington, D.C. and personally confront President Lincoln with what he felt was a gross miscarriage of justice. After hearing his argument, President Lincoln ordered a member of his staff to review the trial records. The staff man concurred with Bishop Whipple's statements and President Lincoln ordered over 250 Indians to be released. Thirty-eight Indians were to be hung, not 300. The Indians were quartered on the snow-swept prairie until the day after Christmas, 1862, when the execution was to take place

The largest mass execution in American history occurred in <u>Mankato</u>, Minnesota on December 26, 1862. People came from miles around to watch the hanging of 38 Indian braves.

The following summer all the Sioux who had survived a severe winter and scarlet fever epidemic were marched to a barren location in the Dakota Territory and told not to return to Minnesota. And so ended the Sioux Uprising.

"I love a people who have always made me welcome to the best they had...who are honest without laws, who have no jails and no poor house...who never take the name of God in vain...who have never raised a hand against me, or stolen my property...where there is no law to punish either..."

> George Catlin, American Artist who lived among the Plains Indians between 1820 and 1838.

"I do not understand why nothing is done for my people. I have heard talk and talk, and nothing is done....It makes my heart sick when I remember...all the broken promises.

> __Chief Joseph

Distance between
<u>Pipestone</u> and
<u>Montevideo</u> is
approximately
82 miles.

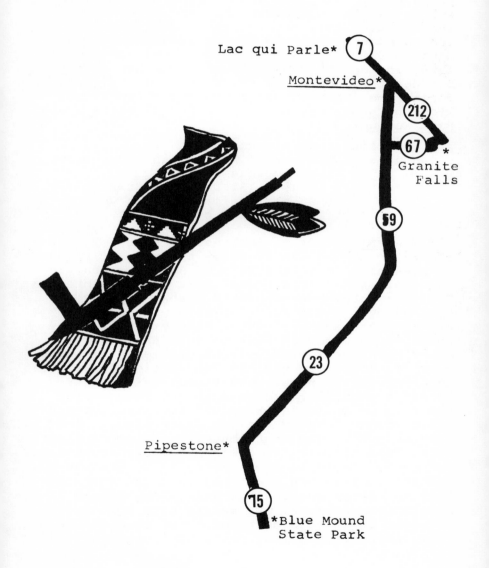

Lac qui Parle* ⑦

Montevideo* ⑳

⑫ 212

⑥ 67

*
Granite
Falls

⑤ 59

㉓ 23

<u>Pipestone</u>*

㊄ 75

*Blue Mound
State Park

NEAR THE
SOUTH DAKOTA
BORDER

Protestant missionaries began to arrive in
Minnesota in the late 1820s. They worked with
the Sioux and Chippewa tribes and by the mid-
1830s were widely regarded as agricultural
teachers and educators of the Indian children.
By the 1830s, the Sioux language had been trans-
lated and communication became somewhat easier
between the Indian and the white man--at least
for a time. A replica of the first Protestant
Mission Chapel may be seen at La qui Parle State
Park Museum.

Location: County Road 13
Hours: Memorial Day to Labor Day from
               10 am to 4 pm
Fees: Adults ($1.00), children (25¢).
               No charge for children when
               accompanied by a parent.

Montevideo has an interesting past. In the
1700s, this land was owned by the King of France.
He presented it to the King of Spain. Then, in
1870, after the area became part of the Minnesota
Territory, the beginnings of a town appeared on
the surveyor's records. In 1879, there was a
village here and by 1908, a city existed. Many
townspeople wondered what to name their city.
After much consideration, one gentleman recalled
a visit to Uruguay and the land's ties to Spain.
He proposed the name, Montevideo, which means
"I see a mountain." More than 200 years after
the King of Spain had received the land, communication began between the two Montevideos. The
Uruguan Montevideo contributed a statue of their
hero, Juan Artigas, to their Minnesota counterpart
and gifts travelled from Minnesota to Uruguay.
Perhaps in only one small way, a rural American
town has shown the way to make international
neighborliness work. We salute both Montevideos
and hope their ties continue to strengthen and
that other communities follow their lead.

Granite Falls has been built on a bluff overlooking the Minnesota Valley. The rocks along
the sides of the Minnesota River were formed so
long ago that experts claim they date back to
the oldest era of Minnesota's geological history.

Besides antique rocks, come to Granite Falls
and see a handsome collection of antique automobiles at the Yellow Medicine Historical Society
Museum. This museum also features 2 log cabins
and a "model home" showing how the early settlers
lived.

Location: Granite Falls
Hours: Memorial Day to Labor Day from
              1-5 pm, Tuesday through Sunday.
              Closed on Mondays
Fees: Admission charged

PIPESTONE NATIONAL MONUMENT

Location: 1 mile north of the city of
              Pipestone
Hours: Visitor's Center is open year
              round from 8 am to 9 pm (during
              the summer months) and 8 am to
              5 pm (during the winter months)
Fees: Free

When visiting Pipestone National Monument, we
recommend that you make your first stop at the
Visitor's Center. Here, within a small but
excellent museum, much of what you will later see
is detailed and explained. Be sure to spend a
few moments examining the peace pipes at the
right of the entrance.

The Circle Trail begins at the Visitor's
Center. This 3/4 mile, well-marked trail brings
an earlier Indian world into focus for the
20th century visitor. A detailed, descriptive
trail brochure may be borrowed from the Visitor's
Center. It is free for your use, but please
return it so that someone else may walk with it
later.

Pipestone Quarry is reserved for Indians by Federal law. This national monument affords a wonderful opportunity for an afternoon of becoming better acquainted with tribal customs and culture. In addition to the quarries, this is one of southwestern Minnesota's best preserved areas of natural beauty.

For at least 300 years, a large proportion of the Plains Indians' ceremonial pipes were produced from the unusual stone quarried at Pipestone. The stone was an object of reverence and was held in awe by all Indian tribes.

Ceremonial pipes, peace pipes, or calumets (as they were sometimes called), were highly valued. Indians believed that the greatest misfortune would occur to anyone who broke the words of a treaty after having smoked the peace pipe.

George Catlin, an American artist who lived among the Plains Indians from the 1820s to 1838 wrote:

"...Many ages after the red men were made, when all the different tribes were at war, the Great Spirit sent runners and called them all together at the 'Red Pipe.'--He stood on the top of the rocks, and the red people were assembled in infinite numbers on the plains below. He took out of the rock a piece of the red stone, and made a large pipe; he smoked it over them all; told them that it was part of their flesh; that though they were at war, they must meet at this place as friends; that it belonged to them all; that they must make their calumets from it and smoke them to him whenever they wished to appease him or get his good-will-- the smoke from his big pipe rolled over them all, and he disappeared in its cloud."

We particularly enjoy a visit to Pipestone in the Spring when the prairie flowers are in blossom and again during a late July/early August weekend to watch the <u>Hiawatha Pageant</u>.

Location: Just outside the Pipestone
                National Monument area, 1 mile
                north of the city of Pipestone
Hours: Last 2 weekends in July, 1st week-
                end in August.
Fees: Admission charged

Many Indian relics are assembled at the <u>Pipestone Historical Museum</u>. There are some interesting petroglyphs (early Indian paintings on stone) to see.

Location: 113 S. Hiawatha Ave., Pipestone
Hours: Daily during the summer months
Fees: Admission charged

A small herd of buffalo make their home at the <u>Blue Mound State Park</u>.

Location: Hwy. 75 a few miles north of Rt.
                90.
Hours: Daily
Fees: Permit required. See p. 124.

OLD TOWNS NEW TOWNS

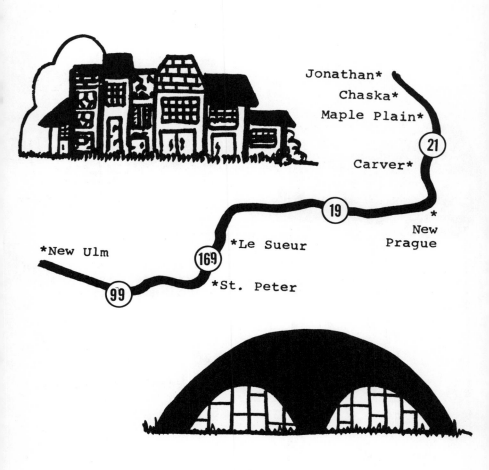

Jonathan*

Chaska*

Maple Plain*

(21)

Carver*

(19)

New
Prague

*Le Sueur

*New Ulm

(169)

(99)

*St. Peter

Southcentral Minnesota provides a wonderful
range of contrasts only 80 miles from the Twin
Cities. Take a few hours to explore a town
recently off the architect's drawing boards, a
town which is being restored through the untiring
efforts of a group of ladies, a town which was
under siege for 3 days during the Indian Uprising,
a town which once thought it would become
Minnesota's capitol city--and more!

Jonathan is a new town. Only a few years
ago this community was a patchwork of fields and
farmhouses. The land was purchased and a group
of businessmen began to think of a community
where each resident would be able to leave his
home via either a walking, horseback riding, or/and
auto route. Within this self-contained community
they envision individual and multi-dwelling units,
stores, churches, schools, and industries.
Although much of Jonathan is still in the planning
stage, we enjoy watching its progress.

    Location: Near Chaska, Rt. 41.

The Minnesota Arboretum is a pleasure to visit
throughout the year. If you are beginning to
landscape a home, a visit here is a must. For,
within the Arboretum's extensive grounds, all
plants and trees which grow well in Minnesota
have been planted and labeled. For the casual
visitor, we particularly recommend a spring visit
to see the Wildflower Garden.

    Location: State Hwy. 5 between Chanhassen
                 and Victoria
    Hours: Daily from 8 am to sunset
    Fees: Free, except for weekend car fee.

SW-Maple Plain, Carver

At first glance, the <u>Ensculptic House</u> staggers
the imagination. This revolutionary, free-form
polyurethane and fiberglas home reflects a new
direction for home construction. Housewives will
enjoy seeing the workfree details while most men
marvel at the planning that went into the
building's construction.

Location:	200 C West Branch Road, Rt. 2, Maple Plain
Hours:	Tours given by appointment only. Arrangements may be made by telephoning 479-2633
Fees:	$1.50 per person

<u>Carver</u> is a special community. In the late
1960s, a small group of dedicated women formed
a committee and began to stop the deterioration
of a 19th century Minnesota River town. The
preservation, restoration, and beautification
of Carver-on-the-Minnesota continues at an
exciting pace.

Location:	1 mile west of Chaska on Hwy. 212, turn left onto Co. Rd. 40 and proceed about 3/4 mile to Carver
Hours:	Group tours of the restored buildings are planned 4-5 times a year. Phone (on Monday mornings) for details: 448-3436
Fees:	$1.50 per person for the guided tour.
Note:	Try to attend Carver's Steamboat Jubilee in September. It's fun!

Once there was an old hotel. It had been
neglected for many years when a family came to
live in it. The family worked hard. The wife
arranged with some of the nearby farmwives to
purchase the best and freshest fruits and vege-
tables available. With a small group of helpers,
she began to preserve and can and pickle all sorts
of good things to eat. All these cans and jars
were stored in the hotel's basement.

Meanwhile, people began to come to eat at the
New Prague Hotel. They told their friends about
the Victorian dining room with antiques for sale,
the roast duck, and the 5" high lemon merangue
pie. But most of all, they told about the happy
feeling within this small hotel. Save a Sunday
afternoon for a leisurely drive to New Prague
and the hotel that came back.

Location: Main Street, New Prague
Hours: Daily

There is a small community which came to
national prominence in the 1950s when a marvelous
advertising campaign reminded us all of the
Jolly Green Giant's home--Le Sueur.

The highlight of the town's summer season
comes in Mid-August with Corn on the Curb Days.
Steam engines and tons of fresh corn make a
butter drenched day to remember.

Location: High School Ball Field, Le Sueur
Hours: Mid-August. Write to the Chamber
            of Commerce for specific dates
Fees: Free, although you are encouraged
            to buy a Booster Button for $1.00.
            This entitles you to all the corn
            you can eat over a 3 day period.

St. Peter is one of Minnesota's loveliest cities. Once expected to become the state's capitol, it was planned with wide boulevards and planted with stately trees. One of the most interesting places to visit in town is Gustavus Adolphus College.

Location:	West Hill, St. Peter
Hours:	Daily
Fees:	Free
Note:	Modernistic Christ Chapel is beautifully illuminated at night.

There are Indian artifacts and historical items at the Nicollet County Historical Museum.

Location:	400 S. 3rd St., St. Peter
Hours:	Monday through Friday from 2-5 pm Closed on holidays
Fees:	Free

New Ulm was founded by the Turner Society--a group of Germans who were devoted to developing body and mind. The town retains a distinctively Germanic character and is well worth a leisurely visit.

The children always ask to visit Herman the German's Statue. He united the German tribes in 9 AD by defeating the Roman army's attempt to dominate Germany. The 102' tall structure dominates the city's hillside and, from the base, affords a lovely view of the city.

Reminders of New Ulm's Indian Uprising Days will be found throughout the city. However, be sure to stop at the Brown County Hist. Soc. Museum to learn more about the lives of the settlers and the Indians.

Location: Broadway and 1st Street, North

Our favorite building in New Ulm is the <u>Post Office</u>!

AN
ABBREVIATED
DINING
GUIDE

Afton, Afton Inn (NE)

Brainerd, *Lumbertown
  Dining Room, Prime
  Rib Room [Madden Inn] (NW)

Duluth, The Flame, London
  House (NE)

Grand Rapids, Rainbow Inn (NW)

Itasca, *Douglas Lodge (NW)

Little Falls, Pine Edge Inn (NW)

Lutsen Resort Dining Room (NE)

Mankato, Century Club, Michael's
  (SW)

Mantorville, Hubbel House (SE)

Minneapolis, Camelot, Charlie's,
  Harry's, Rosewood Room [North-
  star Inn] (TC)

New Prague Hotel (SW)

Park Rapids, *Rapid River
  Logging Camp (NW)

Red Wing, *Nybo's (SE)

Rochester, Elizabethan Room
  [Kahler Hotel], Michael's (SE)

St. Cloud, Griffin Room
  [Germain Hotel], (NW)

St. Paul, Blue Horse, Lindey's,
  McColl Pub, Top of the
  Hilton (TC)

St. Peter, Gannons (SW)

Stillwater, The Lowell Inn (NE)

Two Harbors, Two Sisters (NE)

*Particularly fun with children.

Spend a few days paddling quietly through the Boundary Waters Canoe Area, catch a pan-full of perch and eat them before a roaring campfire as the sky provides a kaleidoscope of impressions. Breathe deeply and understand the scent of pine and earth and fresh air.   THIS IS RECREATION IN MINNESOTA.

Park in the largest stadium lot in the middle west and join the excited fans streaming toward the building. Find your way to a comfortable seat and nibble popcorn as the tension builds on the ice below you. Watch high school talent compete fiercely for the coveted championship--a championship for which every school in the state has been working. THIS IS RECREATION IN MINNESOTA.

Walk quietly along a river bank, binoculars and camera in hand. Pause a moment to focus on the sound of spring returning to a melting countryside. The birds are back, the woods are alive with the first twinge of green sprouting from the long-dormant branches. The lady slipper nudges the earth and you walk on to see what spring exists around the silent bend of a path. THIS IS RECREATION IN MINNESOTA.

Come to the lake this weekend! Everyone is enjoying the water. Sailboat races are happening in one corner, houseboat picnics spot the lake, and waterskiing, fishing, canoeing, swimming can be seen. The lake is busy. We'll come again in wintertime when all is quiet. Arrive in mid-afternoon on a cold, crisp, sunlit day. Ice houses dot the lake, snowmobile races are happening in one corner, sled dog races in another, an ice hockey game is in progress and children are having sliding races. There's even an ice boat under full sail. This lake is in use all year round. THIS IS RECREATION IN MINNESOTA.

FUN YEAR PARK ENTRANCE PERMIT $3.00
WEEKEND PARK ENTRANCE PERMIT $1.00

Minnesota has a vast, varied, and beautiful selection of state parks. One of the biggest bargains available to the state's tourist is an annual state park entry permit. It may be purchased at the entrance to any Minnesota state park. Buy it and use it! Join the fun!

We include the following compilation of state park facilities which may be of assistance as you begin to plan a weekend trip.

STATE PARKS/FACILITIES	Picnicking	Beach	Nature Trails	Museum	Fishing	Camp Grounds	Boats/Canoes	Group Camp	Childrens Trails	Snowmobile
Banning	x		x		x	x				
Baptism River	x		x		x					
Bear Head Lake	x	x	x		x	x	x			
Beaver Creek Valley	x		x		x	x				
Big Stone Lake	x	x			x	x				
Birch Coulee	x		x							
Blue Mound	x	x	x		x	x				
Buffalo River	x	x	x		x	x				x
Camden	x	x	x		x	x		x		x
Caribou Falls			x		x					
Carley	x		x		x					
Cascade River	x		x		x	x				
C.A. Lindburgh	x		x	x	x					
Crow Wing	x		x		x	x				x
Father Hennepin	x	x	x		x	x				
Flandrau	x		x		x	x		x		x
Forestville	x		x		x	x				x
Fort Ridgeley	x		x	x						x
Fort Snelling	x	x	x	x	x					x
Frontenac	x		x			x				x
Glacial Lakes	x	x			x	x				

MINNESOTA'S STATE PARK FACILITIES

	Picnicking	Beach	Nature Trails	Museum	Fishing	Camp Grounds	Boats/Canoes	Group Camps	Children's Trails	Snowmobile Trails
Gooseberry Falls	x		x		x	x				
Helmer Myre	x		x		x	x				x
Interstate	x		x	x	x	x	x			
Itaska	x	x	x	x	x	x	x	x		x
Jay Cooke	x		x		x	x				x
Magney	x		x		x	x				
Kilen Woods	x		x		x	x				
Kodonce River	x		x							
Lac qui Parle	x	x	x	x	x	x				
Lake Bemidji	x	x			x	x	x			
Lake Bronson	x	x	x		x	x	x	x		x
Lake Carlos	x	x	x		x	x	x	x		x
Lake Louise	x	x	x		x					x
Lake Maria	x		x							
Lake Shetek	x	x	x	x	x	x	x	x		x
Maplewood	x	x	x		x	x				x
McCarthy Beach	x	x	x		x	x	x			
Mille Lacs-Kathio	x	x	x	x	x	x				x
Minneopa	x		x		x					
Monson Lake	x		x		x	x				
Nerstrand Woods	x		x			x				x
Old Mill	x	x	x	x	x	x				
Rice Lake	x		x			x				
St. Croix	x	x	x	x	x	x	x	x		x
Sakatah Lake	x	x	x		x	x				
Savanna Portage	x	x	x		x	x				x
Scenic	x	x	x	x	x	x	x			x
Schoolcraft	x		x		x	x				
Sibley	x	x	x		x	x	x	x		x
Split Rock Creek	x	x			x	x				
Split Rock Lighthouse	x		x							
Temperance River	x		x		x	x				
Tower Soudan	x		x	x	x					x
Traverse de Sioux	x		x		x					
Upper Sioux Agency	x		x	x						
Whitewater	x	x	x		x	x			x	
William O'Brien	x	x	x		x	x	x			
Zippel Day	x	x			x	x				

Table courtesy of the Minnesota Highway Department.

CANOEING

You could almost canoe through Minnesota!

Sixteen of Minnesota's loveliest canoeing rivers are shown below, as well as the BWCA (see pp. 10-13).

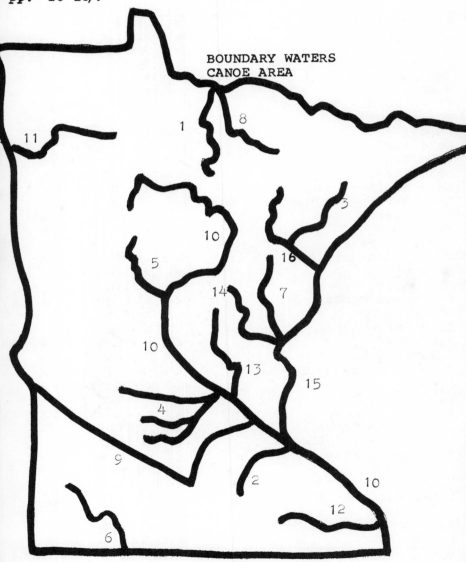

BOUNDARY WATERS CANOE AREA

The canoe rivers shown on the opposite page are:

1.	Big Fork	9.	Minnesota
2.	Cannon	10.	Mississippi
3.	Cloquet	11.	Red Lake
4.	Crow	12.	Root
5.	Crow Wing	13.	Rum
6.	Des Moines	14.	Snake
7.	Kettle	15.	St. Croix
8.	Little Fork	16.	St. Louis

The State of Minnesota has published an excellent 48 page paperback describing the access points, camp sites, mile markings, river flow, rapids, historic sites, etc. concerning the above mentioned 16 rivers. The brochure is entitled <u>Minnesota Voyageur Trails</u> (paperback, $2.00, The Documents Section, 140 Centennial Building, St. Paul, Minnesota 55101). It is very helpful for use when planning a canoeing vacation!

Minnesota has over 420 private and municipal camping areas, approximately 1,650 campsites which are accessible from the water, 65 campgrounds in national forests, more than 150,000 acres of State Park land, over 2,933,310 acres of State Forest land, and over 10,000 lakes within the wilderness canoeing area. There is a place for you to camp in Minnesota! And, if you like to be alone, there are literally thousands of places to stake your tent where you probably won't see another human being for weeks.

Campsite fees vary in municipal and private campgrounds. Within the Minnesota State Parks, the charge is $2.00 per campsite per night.

CAMPING

Campsites are assigned on a first come, first served basis for not more than a 2 week period. A yearly admission permit to ALL of Minnesota's state parks costs $3.00.

The glove compartment of every Minnesota camper's car should contain:

<u>Minnesota! A Camper's Guide and Map</u>

This superb reference phamphlet is available free of charge by writing to the Minnesota Department of Economic Development, 57 West 7 Street, St. Paul, Minnesota 55101,

BOATING

Boating is a tremendously popular pastime in Minnesota. To increase your fun on the water, we recommend the following free publications:

Lake Map Index (paperback, Documents Section, 140 Centennial Bldg., St. Paul, Minn. 55101). This lists all the contour lake maps, alphabetically by county, for the entire state. The maps must be ordered separately and cost $1.00, but the index is free.

U.S. Coast Guard Regulations (paperback, The Commissioner, 2nd Coast Guard District, St. Louis, Mo.). Coast Guard regulations apply to the Mississippi, the Minnesota River, the St. Croix River, and boundary waters between adjacent states and Canada.

Minnesota, Synopsis of Boat and Water Safety Laws (paperback, Dept. of Conservation, 625 N. Robert St., St. Paul, Minn. 55101).

Registration fees for boats in Minnesota waters are:

Boats under 26 feet   - $ 5.00
Boats over 26 feet   -   10.00

We spoke with water safety patrol officers throughout the state and pass on these comments

1. Be careful of gasoline. Less than 1/2 cup of gasoline can do as much damage as 6 sticks of dynamite.

2. Do not overcrowd your boat--do not overpower a boat.

3. Remember to display a light or lantern on your boat(that is visible 2 miles away)--no matter what the size of the boat may be--when out at night. One of the major causes of "accidents" is being run down by patrols which are on the way to an emergency. Keep the lights on at night so you can be seen!

129

Drive safely. Know and heed the "road signs"
of Minnesota's beautiful lakes and rivers.
These markers are just one of the continuing
services being provided by the Minnesota Department
of Conservation. By understanding and complying
with these markers, <u>you</u> may help lower the number
of fatalities on Minnesota waterways.

Do <u>not</u> anchor your boat on buoys!

Swim   Area

<u>Diamond Shape with Cross</u> means
boats keep out.

Rock

<u>Diamond Shape</u> warns of
danger.

<u>Diver's Flag</u> indicates
presence of diver (who is
probably underwater).

<u>All black buoy</u> in-
dicates boat should
pass between it and
its companion <u>all
red buoy</u>.

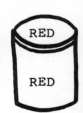

RED

RED

Square or rectangle gives
information, names,
distances, activities,
etc.

Circle means controlled
area "as indicated."

Black topped white buoy
indicates boat should pass
to NORTH or EAST.

Red topped white buoy
indicates boat should pass
to SOUTH or WEST.

Anchor buoy.

Red striped white buoy
indicates boat should not
pass between buoy and
nearest shore.

FISHING

Minnesota has over 15,290 fresh-water lakes (which are over 10 acres in size), 1,900 miles of trout streams and 13,100 miles of inland rivers. That provides room for a lot of fish and a lot of fishermen. Each year, over 25 million pounds of fresh-water fish are taken from the waterways by tall-tale-telling fishing enthusiasts. The big difference is that in Minnesota, the tall tales are often true. Come fish here and find out for yourself.

Seasons, limits, license fees and all other regulations pertaining to the taking of fish in Minnesota is controlled by the Minnesota Department of Conservation. Licenses are required. They may be purchased through county agents, resort operators, sporting goods stores, etc. The license fees for 1971 are:

Individual (resident)	$ 4.00
Combination (", husband and wife)	6.00
Individual (non-resident)	6.00
Individual (" , 3 days)	3.00
Combination (" , husband and wife)	10.00

Contour maps of over 3,000 fishing lakes are available. See page 11 for details.

Minnesotans never stop fishing. In 1970, the ice house population on Mille Lacs Lake was larger than the resident population of Silver Bay. More than a million pounds of fish were caught through the ice in 1970. No wonder ice fishing has become such a popular pastime!

Most Minnesotans guard their "special" fishing sites with great fervor. We've heard of fishing lakes being willed to loved ones. However, if you're new to the Minnesota fishing world, ask a sporting goods dealer, a game warden, or at one of the fish management field stations. No-one leaves a Minnesota fishing vacation without LOTS OF FISH.

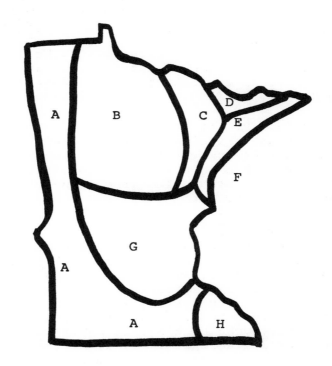

Region A - Bullhead, rough fish

Region B - Hard water walleye

Region C - Soft water walleye

Region D - Lake trout

Region E - Stream trout

Region F - Smelt

Region G - Bass, panfish

Region H - Stream trout

IN MINNESOTA, YOU NEVER JUST CATCH "A FISH!"

SOME
GOOD
FISHING
SPOTS

Bullhead

The "Bullhead Capital of the World" is
located in and around Waterville, Minnesota.
Lake Tetonka and Sakatah are exceptionally
good spots to fish for this delicious morsel.

Northern Pike

Spider Lake, near Grand Rapids, and Big
Mantrap, near Park Rapids, are two of the best
spots for this powerful fighting fish. The
largest Northern pulled from Minnesota waters
was over 45 pounds!

Muskellunge (Muskies)

Leech Lake, Rainy Lake, Lake of the Woods
and, in general, the north central portion of
the state. It is sometimes difficult for all
but the most avid anglers to tell a Muskie from
a Northern. The never-fail method is by counting
the sensory pores under the lower jaw. If the
fish you've caught has 5 or fewer pores on each
side, it's a Northern. If it has more than 5
pores on each side, it's a Muskie. We'll leave
it to you to locate the sensory pores!

Bass

Smallmouth - The Minnesota-Canadian border
lakes area is considered one of the best smallmouth areas in the world. Rainy Lake is a good
location.

Largemouth - Alexandria, Grand Rapids, Park
Rapids, Fergus Falls, Minnetonka--all offer
excellent largemouth bass fishing. Use a light
fly rod and be prepared for some excitement!
The record largemouth weighed almost 15 pounds.

Trout

   Lake - Superb lake trout fishing (and superb scenery) will be found along the Gunflint Trail. It will be found in many of the deeper lakes in the northeastern section of the state.

   Stream - Rainbows, large browns, and brook trout are found along the North Shore of Lake Superior. The area near the Knife River is very popular. The Whitewater River in southern Minnesota, the Straight River near Park Rapids, and the St. Croix tributaries are also good fishing spots for stream trout.

   The Minnesota Conservation Department has published an excellent Guide to Lakes Managed for Stream Trout. We recommend that you write for it and Trout Streams of Minnesota (paperbacks, free, Minnesota Department of Economic Development, 57 West 7th Street, St. Paul, Minnesota 55102).

Panfish

   Panfish are all over. However, many anglers seem to prefer the areas near Park Rapids, Detroit Lakes, and Alexandria.

   Have fun, find fish, and enjoy the state's beautiful scenery as you quietly sit and wait for the BIG ONE.

SMELT
FEVER

Sometime between April 14 and 29 the excitement builds along the shores of Lake Superior and the smelt watch is on!

Once the smelt have been sighted, word travels quickly. Thousands of smelters begin to line the sandy ridge at Duluth's Park Point and at the mouths of streams and rivers along the lower portion of Lake Superior's North Shore.

Most smelting is done at night, when the water is alive with the small, silvery fish.

The fish are caught with nets, buckets, 25' long seines, by hand, in boot, or with almost any other implement which will contain them. The scene is unbelievable.

During a good "run," over a hundred pounds of fish can be dipped from the water in only a few minutes. That's fishing!

About 1 million pounds of smelt are taken by sport fishermen in Minnesota each year.

⊕   Regional headquarters

+   Area headquarters

●   Substations

Trout and salmon rearing stations

    Visitors are welcome to visit the fish rear-
ing pools. A number of them are discussed in
detail in other sections of the book.

HUNTING

Many Minnesotans await the start of the hunting season with more enthusiasm than little boys have waiting for Santa Claus!

We hope the following maps will assist you in "the hunt."

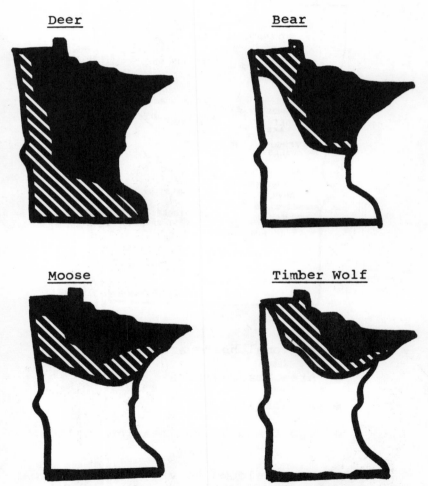

Solid black means animal is common in area. Shaded area signifies animal is present, but not in large numbers.

Beaver

Cottontail Rabbit

Jack Rabbit

Gray Fox and Gray Squirrel

Woodcock

Hungarian Partridge

Sharp-tailed Grouse

Pheasant

Prairie Chicken

Ruffled Grouse

The state provides some excellent reference materials for hunters. All of the following may be purchased through the Documents Section, 140 Centennial Building, St. Paul, Minnesota 55101.

<u>Big Game in Minnesota</u> (paperback, $2.50)

<u>White-tailed Deer of Minnesota</u> (paperback, $2.50)

<u>Timber Wolf in Minnesota</u> (paperback, $1.15)

<u>The Beaver in Minnesota</u> (paperback, $1.15)

In addition, <u>fire plan maps</u> are available for most of the state's heavily wooded areas. These maps show all roads, lakes, streams, trails, railroad grades, ponds, and other details, including the location of power transmission lines. Most maps cover approximately 36 square miles or about 23,000 acres. Indexes to available maps are free of charge from the Documents Section (see address on opposite page). The maps cost 50¢ each. This is another of the state's exceptional bargains.

Hunting licenses are required and may be purchased from any county agent. The Fees are:

Resident small game	$5.00
Resident bow and arrow, deer	7.50
Resident deer firearm	7.50
Resident trapping	$3.00
Non-resident small game	26.00
Non-resident deer bow and arrow	10.25
Non-resident deer firearm	50.25

When obtaining your licence, be sure to ask for a copy of the <u>Hunting and Trapping Regulations</u>. They list laws in effect and give season information for each animal in the state. The brochure is also fun to read while waiting for the season to start!

Hidden
Valley*

Buena
Vista
*

Red
Lake
Falls
*

Giant's*
Ridge

Lutsen*

Val*
Chatel

*Sugar
Hills

*
Mount
Rockwood

*Quadna

*
Detroit
Mt.

Ski*
Gull

*French
Rapids

see
next
page
→

Hole-
in-
*the-
Mt.

*
Ski
Haven

Little*
Squaw

142

Metropolitan Twin Cities Ski Locations

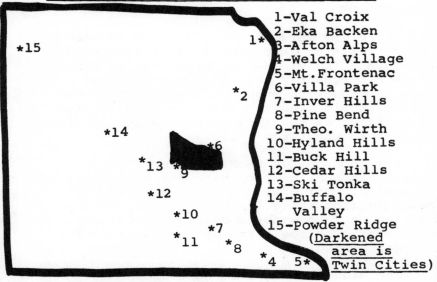

1-Val Croix
2-Eka Backen
3-Afton Alps
4-Welch Village
5-Mt.Frontenac
6-Villa Park
7-Inver Hills
8-Pine Bend
9-Theo. Wirth
10-Hyland Hills
11-Buck Hill
12-Cedar Hills
13-Ski Tonka
14-Buffalo
   Valley
15-Powder Ridge
   (Darkened
    area is
    Twin Cities)

The Ski Information Service offers weather and snow information for Minnesota, parts of Canada, Wisconsin, and Michigan. Phone: 645-5551. The Service requests callers to ask about no more than 3 locations per call.

The Minnesota State Highway Patrol provides highway condition reports. Within the Twin Cities area, the number is 221-3076.

SNOWMOBILING

There are more than 2,400 miles of snow-mobile trails on state and federal land within Minnesota. The Minnesota Department of Conservation has recently published an excellent Guide to Minnesota Snowmobiling. Every snow-mobiler should send for this free publication which describes the thousands of miles of snow trails throughout the state.

All snowmobiles in Minnesota, whether operated on public or private property, must be registered. Official application forms are available from state license centers, county sheriffs, and snowmobile dealers throughout Minnesota. The registration fee is $8.00 for a 3 year period.

The Minnesota Department of Economic Development recently released the following information concerning snowmobiling in wilderness areas of the state.

"It is a good idea to leave word at the hotel, motel or resort at which you are staying, spelling out the route you expect to take and your estimated return time.

"Few experienced people go into the wilderness alone. It is good sense to travel in a group; if one machine breaks down, the riders can double up or assist each other for repairs.

"Gasoline which mixes easily with oil in warmer weather tends to stay separated in extreme, sub-zero cold. Care must be taken to insure thorough mixing. Also, a felt strainer is excellent for removing ice crystals from gas cans when refueling on the trail.

"Along with the usual insulated clothing, waterproof boots are essential. The chance of getting into slush is ever present and the ordinary type of felt or leather boot can become quickly soaked. Rubber-bottomed leather boots with half-inch felt liners are preferred foot gear.

"One hazard, seldom considered but very important in the deep, soft snow of wilderness areas, is motor fumes. When a trail has not been broken, snowmobiles may plow through and dig furrows 18 to 25 inches deep. Exhaust fumes tend to stay in the furrows and can cause nausea and severe headaches.

"When breaking trail in deep snow, veteran travellers stop every 15 minutes or so, walk around, sip coffee and check the map.

"To avoid slush or spring holes, it is best to follow established wilderness trails. These can be obtained at no charge from the U.S. Forest Service in Duluth."

GOLF

Clear air and cool breezes make Minnesota golfing a special treat. The following list shows the 18 hole courses throughout the state which are open to the public on a daily fee basis. We have not listed the 9 hole courses-- there are too many! Contact the Chamber of Commerce in the area in which you plan to visit and request full golfing information from them.

Location	Club	All 18 holes Par
Alexandria	Alexandria Golf Club	72
Anoka	Anoka Municipal GC	71
Austin	Ramsey Public GC	71
Bemidji	Town & Country Club	72
Brainerd	Madden Pine Beach Inn	72
Breckenridge	Bois de Sioux	72
Detroit Lakes	Detroit Country Club	71
Duluth	Enger Park Municipal GC	72
"	Lester Park GC	72
Fergus Falls	Pebble Lake Municipal GC	72
Mahnomen	Mahnomen Country Club	72
MINNEAPOLIS AREA		
Edina	Braemar	72
Minneapolis	Columbia GC	65
Eden Prairie	Eden Prairie GC	72
Minneapolis	Francis A. Gross GC	71
Mound	Lakeview GC	69
Hopkins	Meadowbrook GC	72
Plymouth	Hampton	71
Minneapolis	Theodore Wirth GC	69
Pequot Lakes	Breezy Point Estates	71
Rochester	Rochester Golf & Country	71
"	Soldier's Field GC	71
ST. PAUL AREA		
St. Paul	Como Park GC	69
"	Gall's GC	71
"	Highland Park GC	72
"	Keller GC	72
"	Phalen Park GC	65
Virginia	Virginia Municipal GC	70

The following represent but a sampling of
the good times to be enjoyed throughout the
state. Check your newspaper, or write to the
area's Chamber of Commerce, for specific dates.
These are all good fun. Go to them, you'll be
glad you did!

Summer
Corn on the Curb Days, Le Sueur (SW)
Hiawatha Pageant, Pipestone (SW)
Kaffe Fest, Willmar (SW)
Minneapolis Aquatennial (TC)
Minnesota State Fair, St. Paul (TC)
Montevideo Fiesta Days (SW)
Paul Bunyan Water Carnival, Bemidji (NW)
Polka Days, New Ulm (SW)
Steamboat Days, Winona (SE)
Wild Rice Festival, Deer River (NW)

Autumn
Jesse James Days, Northfield (SE)
National Barrow Show, Austin (SW)
Pumpkin Festival, Owatonna (SE)
Steamboat Days, Carver (SW)

Winter
Fairmont Snowmobile Derby (SW)
Hibbing Winter Carnival (NE)
Minnesota Basketball and Hockey Tournaments
   (TC)
St. Paul Winter Carnival (TC)

Spring
Hawk Watch, Duluth (NE)
Apple Blossom Time, La Crescent (SE)
Last Chance Curling Bonspiel, Hibbing (NE)
Smelt Run, Lake Superior (NE)

INDEX

In an attempt to keep this guide current and
helpful, we invite your comments and suggestions.
We would also be grateful for information about
your favorite places throughout Minnesota.

Thank you.

(Cut on the dotted line)

My comments are:

_____

_____

_____

_____

_____

_____

Please mail to:

Tailored Tours Publications
Post Office Box 24222
Minneapolis, Minnesota 55424

Additional copies of
this guide may be
purchased through
your bookseller, or
for $3.25 per copy
(including postage
and handling) from
Tailored Tours
Publications, P.O.
Box 24222, Minneapolis,
Minnesota 55424.